FOOLISH TO BE WISE

Foolish to Be Wise

ROY PEACOCK

KINGSWAY PUBLICATIONS
EASTBOURNE

ISBN 0 86065 343 9

Biblical quotations are from the
Authorized Version (crown copyright).

Front cover photo: Tim Bishopp

**To Elizabeth
whose story this also is
and Matthew
and Rachel
and David**

Printed in Great Britain for
KINGSWAY PUBLICATIONS LTD
Lottbridge Drove, Eastbourne, E. Sussex BN23 6NT by
Cox & Wyman Ltd, Reading.
Typeset by Central Southern Typesetters,
Eastbourne, E. Sussex.

Contents

'Thou, O God, has taught me
from my youth up until now: therefore
will I tell of thy wondrous works'

(Psalm 71:17 *Book of Common Prayer*)

'In the accounts of good men which I have read, I have observed that the writers of them have been partial. They have
given us the bright, but not the dark side of their character.
This, I think, proceeded from a kind of pious fraud, lest mentioning persons' faults should encourage others to sin. It cannot, I am sure, proceed from the wisdom which cometh from
above. The sacred writers give an account of their failings as
well as their virtues. Peter is not ashamed to confess that with
oaths and curses he thrice denied his Master: nor do the Evan-
gelists make any scruple of telling us, that out of Mary Magda-
lene Jesus Christ cast seven devils. I have therefore endeav-
oured to follow their good example. I have simply told what
I was by nature, as well as what I am by grace.'

George Whitefield, introduction
to *A Short Account of God's
Dealings with George Whitefield from
His Infancy to His Ordination
1714–1736*

Prologue

'If you want to get on in life and keep your friends, never discuss politics or religion,' was my father's advice as he saw my inquisitive and discursive nature beginning to develop at the age of fifteen years. So I joined a political party; joining had no effect on my life, but over a number of years steered me well clear of religious things which were, in the event, to have a profound influence.

That early paternal advice had had the heavy implication that not only did nice people not talk about religion, they didn't get involved in it either, but there was a strange contradiction within the home. Neither my father nor mother were churchgoers, but I had been encouraged to go, and when, at a very early age I became a choirboy, my mother accompanied me to church, almost certainly to keep an eye upon me. That I could sing surprised everyone and I progressed eventually to the choir of a church, famous for its choral tradition, in Bristol. It was there that I gained a choral scholarship to the local Cathedral School and it was in that church that I remained until well after my voice had ceased to reach top 'C'. My religious life at that time was Stanford & Stainer, sung to a nicety, missals and masses followed with propriety. So there was for me a strange dichotomy: religion was not a subject for discussion, yet on Sunday it absorbed virtually all of my time.

I am sure that in those teenage years I was not prepared to direct my attention to such incompatibility, although I was increasingly worried that I never sensed any reaction in the God who absorbed my weekend freedom by his demand of my worship. Perhaps this was in keeping with a remote deity, but if he was so remote did it matter much whether I did the right thing or not? Certainly the developing standards of my life did not reflect his interest. Beyond that there was an increasingly gnawing thought that although it was nice to perpetuate a tradition of going to church and to enjoy all the social contacts there, maybe it was otherwise a total waste of time.

Other things thankfully crowded in one those days which were to become a time of excitement as, step by step, I found myself viewing broadening horizons for adventure and mountains of achievement to conquer. As I thought ahead to a career after leaving school, my desire was to become an artist laying oil on canvas. Art had been far and away my best subject, but an unsuspecting world was robbed of a present-day Leonardo when my mother firmly scotched the idea! My uncle had been successful in this field, but the mark of the long years of his early struggle had been left on my mother's mind, and she was not going to allow her son to suffer that way. Earnest discussion led to the decision that, since I liked a pencil in my hand and a drawing board in front of me, perhaps a life as an engineering draughtsman would fill the bill. In this way the mould was cast that would lead to some surprising places.

School-days were followed by a period working in an engineering workshop as a shop-boy: my task was to run errands in general and provide clean hand-cloths for the machinists in particular. A five-year aeronautical engineering apprenticeship followed, when I discovered that, for me, there were more challenging areas of engineering than I had known up to that time. As I began to get a glimpse of what could be achieved, I worked hard to obtain everything available. Four times a week my day would begin at 7.30 a.m. in a workshop and finish at 10.00 p.m. in a night-school class and the other evenings were largely spent in study. Saturday afternoon was for a game of rugby and Sunday brought about the

increasingly dreary act of going to church, made all the
bleaker when compared with the interests in the week.
In the whole of that period I recall just one remark
made in a sermon by an aged priest whom everyone
called Father Gurney. 'It doesn't really matter how dirty
the cup is on the outside so long as it's clean inside.' That
remark perplexed me and for years I wondered what it
meant. Certaintly he was talking at a philosophical level
that I hadn't yet reached and the comparison he used
was by no means clear to me. I did not know that while I
would like to drink from a cup that was clean inside, I
would certainly not choose one that was not clean and
attractive on the outside also: the lips would touch the
outside as well as the inside when I drank, I thought,
but, even more important, the crockery should look
good. Little did I know that my reasoning was really a
parable of my situation: striving to make the outside
look good. This was to come under challenge increasingly as time moved on.

My apprenticeship had brought a crop of prizes, both
the workshop and the lecture-room work having yielded
their harvest, but there loomed the prospect of two years
compulsory military service. I thought of this as an un-
desirable waste of time in a life that could only be lived
once and I was determined to avoid it, not on the
grounds of conscience, but because there had to be a
more exciting world to explore as the mind was expanded
to accommodate it. The bolt-hole I found was to work in
a reserved occupation as it was known, a military defence
project. There was a problem though: this was a permanent haven to those who had a university degree, but
to me, it was my ground cover for only two years.

Those two years were good, awakening my interest in
the mysteries of combustion, chemical kinetics and fluid
mechanics, branches of engineering whose existence
were quite new to me. But my interest was awakened in
other areas, too, as I found myself in the apparently
rarified atmosphere of a set of university graduates all
expressing themselves in ways that were alien to me as a
shop-boy. Every discussion seemed to expand the mind

and the excitement of testing real aero-engines, assuming responsibility for their running and then analyzing the measured data, brought unparalleled delight. After two years the spectre of military service again loomed and there was an even greater determination to avoid wasting time that could be usefully employed in pursuing my emerging career ambitions. So a suggestion that I should go to study at a university came at a welcome moment, but to do a bachelor's degree on top of the experience I already had seemed to be counter-productive, and so I was admitted for a postgraduate degree.

Those were the days when I discovered that a friendship formed a few years before with a girl called Elizabeth was growing in a direction we had not anticipated. When we found that the occasional meeting had become a daily occurrence, a few minutes after nightschool, coffee in a cellar restaurant in Bristol and the increasingly regular walk late at night across the city to get home after the buses had stopped running, we had to admit that we were in love. Plans did not stretch far into the future when we became engaged or even when we were married: for me, the pursuit of academic honour consumed me in a chase whose destiny I couldn't see and for Elizabath, the financial rewards of a teaching career kept us both afloat.

It was at the outset of a short and very unhappy period back in industry that I met Mike. He had been to the same academic institute as me and had then gone on to Cambridge to read for a doctorate in philosophy. I told him how bored I was at the prospect of industry again and, in an off-hand sort of way, he suggested that I might go to Cambridge myself to study for a Ph.D. *Cambridge!* The word was pure magic but the expectation unobtainable. Mike was firm; we would go there for a day and have a look-around and then I should make my decision: if I liked it he would point me in the direction to open the correspondence. In a dream I walked through one or two colleges, along King's Parade and into the engineering laboratory. There I met men who seemed giants to one who had watched with envy the

almost aristocratic behaviour of new graduates in their
reserved occupation in industry. Yet the dream was to
come true: not, I was to discover, for the mind-exercis-
ing purposes and for the career structure that would be
thus shaped, but for a purpose decided by the God who
had been forgotten by the erstwhile choir-boy and altar
server. That God may have seemed, at best, to be remote
— although more likely to be non-existent — but he
was moving the pieces on the chess-board in a strategy as
yet to be recognized, to bring about a challenge that
would defy the detached intellectual assessment I now
thought right and proper for an emergent scientist.

The move to Cambridge brought both the thrill of a
new life to explore and the relief that something from
the past could be quietly dropped. The emptiness of our
church-life had only been improved somewhat by the
social relationships that it generated and now that these
friends were on the other side of England there was no
natural church contact. We found that all church-related
activities could be avoided without hurting anybody, but
perhaps more important, without facing the intellectual
challenge of trying to reconcile the irreconcilable feature
of our past lives — worshipping a God whom I frankly
no longer believed was there.

The time to leave Cambridge approached. A job at
the aero-engine company Rolls-Royce Limited beckoned
me and life was set fair as I surveyed my world: Elizabeth,
two children, a house and five cars. I know that many
people have a confrontation with the Lord God when
everything has fallen about their ears, some are in
prison, others in the clutches of social evils, but for me
that moment came when everything looked good, not
bad. But thus it had to be, for mine was not to be a battle
with circumstances but a battle with the mind — where
nothing else mattered.

The moment came quite unexpectedly and a small
thing began a disturbance that didn't decay but grew to
a magnitude that would rock my life and change the
destiny for which I worked.

A course was going to be charted physically across

continents and spiritually through experiences of God's hand and power both in career and communion with him. I little knew that, at the same time as through prayer my career blossomed to the point that I was on the faculties of two postgraduate universities — in one of which I held a Research Chair in aeronautics — I would be challenged again and again at the most fundamental level as, with my wife, I stumbled upon the supernatural acts of God. It was a scientist's eyes, trained to quantify observable phenomena, that saw the sick healed, legs grow, cancer go, ears open, lame walk, demons expelled and even a witch fly in a Christian meeting. It was in that scientist, that the battle of the mind was joined one morning in an office in Cambridge University, raged and continues to rage. It was that mind that quarrelled with the Bible, yielding inch by inch as the total reasonableness of the gospel message won his heart, yet fighting a last-ditch battle over the apparently ludicrous story of the Genesis creation only to realize that he was denying the fundamental laws of thermodynamics upon which the whole of his scientific discipline rested.

But even that was only the beginning, for the challenge of the Lord came yet stronger and the words 'Follow me' assumed new significance as, having declined my father's advice in the matter of politics it was now discovered impossible to agree to it in the matter of religious silence. Knowledge is gained that it might be spread and a list of scientific publications from my laboratory bears witness to that principle. The knowledge gained in that laboratory would have a usefulness for a time before it would in all probability be superseded by better data and improved models: the knowledge gained in the laboratory of a life in the hand of God would not lose its desired effects but have eternal merit and it is that knowledge that is embedded in these pages. Paul agonized 'that I may know him' and, as the battle of Paul's mind was continuing when he wrote to the Philippians twenty-six years after his Damascus Road experience, so too there continues the engagement of the mind of the rational man in conflict with the overwhelming evidence of the supernatural God.

The only conclusion that I can reach is that, in Christian matters, it is foolish to be wise, for the wisdom of man cannot compare with that of God. Yet to gain the wisdom of God the rational man has to become, in the world's eyes at least, foolish. It may be foolish to be wise, but to become wise it is necessary to be foolish.

1

Beginnings

Autumn had always been a time of excitement for me: colours changed, leaves fell and suddenly there was the annually renewed experience of toast made on a fork before an open fire, as well as a new realism as dusk enshrouded our games of cops and robbers. But it wasn't the trivial matter of jumping into piles of dead leaves that came to make that period of the year so special — autumn came to represent for me, not just a change of season but a change of lifestyle. I had started school in the autumn, not at the statutory age of five years but at seven because of continuing illness, so my memory of that time remains the sharper. I had moved to a grammar school, a host of new associated experiences, the first game of rugby, the initial entry to a gymnasium, the first — and almost the last — despairing attempt to master Latin declensions and much more, all in the autumn. My working life had started in the autumn when I first put on engineering overalls and began clocking in to a job as dawn was breaking. It was in an autumn that Elizabeth and I looked forward for the first time to the prospect of married life together, when I went to an academic institution, taking on the life of a student and then another autumn when I went on to Cambridge.

So the soft colours, the sun low in the sky, the unexpectedly crisp weather, interspersed with the damp smell of rotting leaves, had all come to mean that change was on the way and, just as I've reacted ever since to those sensory changes, so it was that year when I went up to

Cambridge to pursue the ultimate postgraduate degree. In a life that was becoming increasingly objective and less subjective in its content, it is strange to recognize that, as I entered the period in which only what was objective was significant, I was still subjectively affected by the change of season — and still am.

It was certainly a year of change both for my career and also my personal life. The Cathedral School with its tradition dating from its noble founder, King Henry VIII, had always been a point of stability. Going to work for one of the largest engineering corporations in the United Kingdom had meant exchanging one form of stability for another, but to go to Cambridge had meant stepping away from the stability and risking all on my success or otherwise as a student. That had seemed an enormous step: I little guessed that, as a step, it would initiate the most unexpected changes in my life, which meant that there would be steps to take that made this seem rather small in terms of risk.

The move to Cambridge also coincided with a big change for Elizabeth and me. We had been married for three years and as I prepared for postgraduate life at university, Matthew was born. I assumed the role of a parent in an unusual way — by going to a motor speed-trial in a very fast motor car as part of my emerging, and quite consuming, interest in cars.

That day not only marked the birth of my son but one of those motoring incidents which were to become part of my normal life-style — the whole of the exhaust system of the car dropped off in a quiet Somerset village. We abandoned in a hedge the hot rusting metal to pick it up on our return journey after cooling down, proceeding to our destination in an ear-shattering and quite illegal manner. To our surprise the noise impressed the numerous police officers we passed with the thought, not that we were illegal motorists, but competitors at the speed trial. We were thus directed with the courtesy of salutes to the competitors' enclosure where we had the best view of the proceedings.

That autumn was thus filled with change — a son over

whom I could fuss in the day when he was awake and groan in the night when he didn't sleep, the stability of my employment gone and new horizons of challenge. Everything assumed a secondary significance to those new horizons for, though my background and nature had been very conservative, I was finding a questing within which met a pursuit after knowledge. I had no idea in my mind about where it would lead, but the thrill of this chase was more important than the claim of the prize.

My earlier walk through Cambridge had been as an outsider looking in. I had been a tourist, not ready to spend money for a memento of an ancient city, but willing to spend myself for I knew not what. Now I was on the inside, still walking as in a dream down King's Parade, through Trinity Street and into St John's College, but realizing that the letters addressed to me and waiting in the assigned pigeon-hole in St John's were hard evidence that this was not a dream and I was not an interloper.

Within a day or so of arriving at Cambridge I took a walk to discover this centre of culture and intellect. My eye was soon drawn to a small art gallery whose windows were full of examples of highly coloured abstract paintings on glass behind which a series of electric lights shone.

Fascinated by this strange sight I entered the gallery to be met by a mild little man, balding and in his fifties. He looked more like a commuter, worn down by years of travelling to and from a minor job in an uninteresting office than the artist and creator of these exotica. Soon though he had my ear, his voice rising in excitement while from behind his spectacles his eyes took on the sparkle of a fanatic. Rapidly I was escorted from one room to another, coloured glass leaping to prominence as the bulb behind each piece was switched on. Explanations of what I was looking at poured from my guide and it wasn't until we were in the furthest recesses of the basement that I ventured the incautious remark that I had some difficulty in telling which was the right way up for the pictures.

'What, for instance of that?' I asked pointing at a

sheet of glass about 12″ by 15″. With a total dedication and sense of awe of the masterpiece before us, he took hold of it, held it to the light and asked me,

'But don't you recognize this?'

I had to admit that I didn't, so to settle the matter he announced,

'This way up, it's "The Ploughman Homeward Plods His Weary Way" and this way up,' he added with a theatrical pause as he inverted it, 'it's "Beethoven's Fifth Symphony".'

In that moment I realized that I had arrived at the centre of culture.

Four and a half years at Cambridge as a research student had to be a delight. We had moved to a village ten miles away and daily I drove into the laboratory in one or other of the increasing number of vintage cars that filled the drive and dismayed the neighbours. The comparative poverty of our lives didn't matter much since I was, from early morning to late at night, shaping, so I thought, my own destiny as I explored the behaviour of viscous fluids in parallel curved channels. Little else mattered as I grappled with the solutions of partial differential equations, taught myself vector analysis and then attempted to analyse the three-dimensional fluid data. Morning coffee and afternoon tea in the common room and luncheon in the Granta, the pub across the Backs, were times when we would argue about the behaviour of fluids — how did a turbulent boundary layer become laminar? At times we even ventured into other philosophical domains — why are sand-dunes the shape they are and what are the mechanics of their movement — but one thing we did avoid was any reference to religion, after all, that had been my father's advice.

All of the increasingly intellectual pursuits of life had led to the development of the mind, and the challenges they had brought were for the mind's further development. None had brought a battle, for whenever there had been such a prospect, it had been carefully ignored or sidestepped. So religion was not meant to be discussed, yet at moments it had had to be practised. God's existence had been implicitly assumed in the carefully executed church rites, yet explicitly ignored for the six days of the week that didn't call for religious activity. The growing difficulty of seeing the necessity for any form of deity in an increasingly rationalistic philosophy had been avoided by simply refusing to notice it.

The battle was yet to come, but its moment could only be when I was in a sufficiently polarized position that I could recognize where I was and face the issues squarely. That moment came, when, after four and a half years of Cambridge life, I admitted that I was an agnostic — though in the secrecy of my own heart, I knew that if I assessed my thoughts correctly, mine was the philosophy of an atheist. Such a title I did not covet though: after all, atheists were in all likelihood black-bearded men in wire-rim spectacles, black corduroy trousers and turtle-neck sweaters. They didn't comb their hair in a week because their time was spent marching somewhere to create political trouble — and I'd had enough of politics. So I settled for being an agnostic, so far as my friends were concerned, should they ask me.

★ ★ ★

The room in the engineering laboratory which was to become my daily haunt was also host to a Pole, a South African and a couple of Englishmen, so it carried its own international flavour. We were a curious bunch among whom no real comradeship developed, except with the Pole who couldn't speak English and one Englishman who could.

The Pole, who was a professor in concrete and rein-forced concrete from the Warsaw Institute of Technical Problems, had a name that was quite unpronounceable and a professorial title that always made me think that he might have been the victim of a 1920s Chicago gang killing. I decided to call him George and, to help him get a grasp of the English language, agreed to spend an hour a day going over English words that he had encountered and couldn't understand. In the scientific setting for our discussions these were sometimes quite hilarious. One day, his list of words to be explained included one which in his mid-European gutteral accent he pronounced as *pin-ta* (rhyming with 'winter'). This beat me: it was no engineering term that I had ever encountered, but perhaps because my background was not in the field of civil engineering it was something of specialized application to the esoteric field of reinforced concrete research. After several minutes of grappling with this, I asked George the context in which he had found the word.

'A big sign on a wall' he explained. 'Drinka pinta milka day'.

For his part the Englishman got me interested in the music of Benjamin Britten and my contribution to this cultural exchange was to get him hooked on vintage Riley cars. This turned out to be a mixed blessing for, in due course, I found myself helping to rebuild the engine of a car of his which, when it ran after rebuild, demonstrated the remarkable feature of one forward gear and several in reverse.

The room in which we sat as a body of researchers was not a social centre though, it was a work-house whose peace was only disturbed occasionally by a British army officer on secondment who sang. It wasn't his singing or his other generally noisy ways that particularly disturbed me: he sang songs that were both joyful and religious. I wrote him off as being one of those eccentrics every academic organization must have, if it is to be true to its role cast by the world. Not only did I write him off, I also avoided him because he was likely, at the most unexpected moments, to talk about church.

As a subject for discussion, church was not on my short-list. My father's warnings had left their mark upon me — never discuss religion — and my own church activities over the years had yielded nothing permanent or worthy of discussion. My resultant ignorance left me not questing for knowledge, but running from the subject. When, in fact, my military fellow-student and his wife had us to tea at their house, we were totally perplexed by their conversation: we could not understand their enthusiasm for what, to any right-minded person, seemed nonsense.

Yet it wasn't to meet personalities that I had gone to Cambridge; it was to work. Rapidly, books, papers and articles filled my desk and my life. Elizabeth and the baby Matthew were still in Bristol so my time was divided between the study of, what was to me, a new area of engineering and looking for a house for my geographically divided family. The house hunt finally took me from the town of Cambridge, where we couldn't afford to live, to a village about eleven miles away, Hemingford Grey, where we reckoned we could. The decision to buy a small bungalow was based upon two things: it was cheap and only about twenty minutes drive from the laboratory. That a divine hand could have played a part in that, I was unable to admit for a long while to come, yet Hemingford Grey was to be pivotal in our lives. To live there meant breaking university regulations that I didn't know existed — apparently I had to live within three miles of the porch of Great St Mary's Church — but having made my decision I was not going to change it. After weighty consideration by the university, I was given permission to live in the home I had bought, but I certainly didn't score the last point. I was told that my wife, as my 'lodging-house keeper' had to sign a statement weekly to say that I had arrived home by a certain hour to go to bed — and I was a husband, father and emergent philosopher-scientist!

The days at Cambridge stretched to years and I was happily becoming part of the furniture when it became clear that something had to be done about getting a job. I was so absorbed in my scientific experiments and analysis that such mundane things were not of great interest. Our second child, Rachel, had been born, but my family was a haven to which I turned when fed up with work, not an integral feature of my life. Interest in the world was expressed solely in the growing queue of cars lying in semi-dereliction in the drive and enthusiasm for life outside the laboratory was fully expressed in restoring and rebuilding the ancient engines and bodywork. There was an incident that seemed to reflect well my own sense of priorities when Elizabeth was ill and a doctor had to be called. The bedroom had become the vault for my best car parts and a restored, polished and painted engine stood proudly against the wall. Elizabeth said with feeling that there was no way in which she would see the doctor with an engine in the bedroom, so grudgingly I moved it into the hallway. On arrival at the house the doctor spent twenty enthusiastic minutes examining the engine before examining my wife, whose temper suffered accordingly.

With the apparently approaching end of my Cambridge days it was thus that, mercifully, an interview with the chief scientist of Rolls-Royce Limited led to the invitation to join the Rolls-Royce payroll, but under conditions that I could never have hoped for: I was to stay at Cambridge to develop an idea that I had had in the middle of the interview. Years later, I was to learn that the successful result of that work led to the introduction by Pratt & Whitney, the American aero-engine manufacturers, in a new generation of energy-efficient engines, of the 'Peacock Slot' as it became known. That, though, was not the real reason for the extension of the Cambridge days: the same divine hand that had placed us in Hemingford Grey was preparing us for a revelation of himself that would alter our destiny, but that would happen in his timing.

A point was then reached in my life when it seemed that the years of hard work from that of a shop-boy in an engineering workshop onward were going to be crowned with success. Much had accrued in that period: I had gained a wife, two children, my own home, five cars — and immeasurable experience in rebuilding their engines at the side of the road. Although we were all but penniless, that problem was rapidly being dealt with by regular cheques from Rolls-Royce with whom I now had an appointment beyond the wildest dreams of the sixteen-year-old clocking in to his job, assisting the labourer in a production engineering workshop.

There were more important, yet intangible, products of

those years. The one who had been a rather religious choir-boy and really a quite religious young man serving at an altar, swinging the incense, elevating the chasuble, genu-flecting eastwards, had been liberated from a mythology and had entered the reality of a reasonable world, where intellectual pursuits, widening the horizon of the mind, reigned supreme, so that the mind could be widened yet more. Autumn still brought those emotive and indefinable reactions, yet this was now a life ordered by objective criti-cism to which everything was submitted. Analysis had to be thorough and pursued with a mathematical precision demonstrated in incisive enquiry, comment and conclusion.

The transformation from a religious wide-eyed onlooker to a calculating, atheistic scientist was just about complete and the results were to be known by the world, when George Griffiths came on to the scene. George was every-thing I had intended I would not be and knew I could not be. Retired, according to the rules, he had been an Angli-can priest for all of his life, so far as I knew. Such an exis-tence would never do for me. He lived quietly with his wife in his retirement and quiet living was not my goal. His home was dominated by the glow of polished brass, pol-ished copper and polished wood, every piece having been cared for over centuries as it gained the status of antique. My home was filled with wire furniture, slatted benches and bright simple designs. I might not have liked his tastes but at least I had to admit that his chairs were comfortable.

George was a generation and a half older than me, yet for all our obvious differences I was fascinated by him. He related his interest in old pewter and mentioned how he had sold his collection to pay for a child's education: I wasn't interested in old pewter but I doubted, as I thought about it, that I would be prepared to make that sort of sac-rifice. He talked of antiques, actually firing an interest for them in me and then one day he talked about church. I knew that he would do so eventually, for that had been his lifelong job and the fact that he still wore a clerical collar meant that he must still regard it seriously. For my part, I was already prepared with my strategy: an interest in chess had led me to believe that I should always think one or two moves ahead, so my answer to his suggestion that I might perhaps go to church sometime, came easily.

'George, it's quite impossible. You see, Elizabeth and I have two small babies, we live 120 miles from our nearest family members, we therefore can't arrange baby-sitters, so we can't go to church.' My satisfaction at an entirely reasonable answer delivered with consummate ease was immediately destroyed by his quite unexpected response. 'Oh, that's all right,' he said. 'Once a month we have a crèche on a Sunday morning. You could bring your children along, drop them off at the crèche, then come and enjoy yourself at the church service.' Enjoy myself! It was unthinkable, but equally unthinkable that I didn't seem to have a worthwhile answer for him.

I thought I had been trapped by a man, little realizing that I was being brought, quite unawares, to one of the great points of challenge to be faced in my life. George was a man who no one would want to offend, so I agreed to go to church.

★   ★   ★

Elizabeth's passage over those years had been rather different to mine. She had absorbed herself in caring for the children and saw much less of her husband than was reasonable. She had come from a village atmosphere where her family maintained strong internal interest and relationship. Although her mother died when she was two years old and her father's life had been seriously affected by cancer before an early death, she had always had members of her family around her. Now she was separated from them and nothing had filled the void, certainly not a husband who was more interested in fluid mechanics than family matters. As the years had slipped by, hers had become a lonely life accompanied by a dissatisfaction with herself. Questions of life came to mind in those lonely times and even that of the existence of the God whom she had been trained to acknowledge.

Few friends were made in the village, but among them were Martin and Madeleine with whom we had much in common. Vintage cars filled our conversation with occa-

sional discussion about babies. I enjoyed the former and
ignored the latter.

We had met because Martin, passing our house regularly, had seen my several semi-derelict cars and was finally
drawn to visit us by the sight of a vintage Lagonda in the
drive. The friendship had grown rapidly as he had bought
first a 1926 Humber and then a 3-litre Bentley. The arrival
of the Bentley was cause for Martin to offer Elizabeth a
ride around the country lanes. This, I thought enthusiastically as I watched them disappear around the corner, would
convince my wife of the value and pleasure of real motoring. It didn't work out quite like that though, for within
200 yards a misjudged corner resulted in the Bentley
landing in a deep ditch, causing great embarrassment to
the occupants and amusement to the neighbours. Needless
to say, Elizabeth remained unconvinced.

We soon discovered that Martin and Madeleine went
to church, but although they made the occasional desul-
tory suggestion that we too should go, they weren't considered a threat because they were otherwise quite normal.

The social life, which consisted, in the main, of driving to car rallies for intense conversations on magnetos,
crank-shaft dampers, bulls-eye headlamps and the price
of the specially moulded tyres without which life would
cease was, for Elizabeth, relieved somewhat by occasional
university functions. None was more important than the
May Ball which was held in June and had something to
do, so we were told, with rowing. It was an excuse for an
all-night dance, a surfeit of food, which included swan,
and an ample quantity of champagne. It was too much
of a marathon to face every year, and in any case we
couldn't afford it, but as we scraped the money together,
we would go to celebrate at the end of another academic
year.

Our last May Ball called for a lot of preparation and I
was keen that my wife would be shown off to the best
advantage: there was after all, a certain pride of ownership. Elizabeth eventually emerged for the occasion.
Her hair was carefully set, her make-up perfect and per-
fume just right; her dress was gorgeous. I liked what I

saw as we walked from the house to get into the vintage car of the moment and drive off to the ritual that would carry us well into the next day.

The evening contained for Elizabeth some disturbing features. As I, carrying champagne bottles, squeezed myself time and again through the increasingly noisy crowd, Elizabeth's eyes were arrested by a couple on the dance floor. They bore an air of purity and serenity quite out of place with the surroundings, and as she looked at them she thought that they looked 'clean'. It happened that they were the College Chaplain and his wife.

Upon her return home, Elizabeth caught a glimpse of herself in the mirror. The memory of that couple on the dance floor remained with her as she surveyed, by comparison, her make-up and hair-do. 'I don't like you,' she thought, viewing the picture in the mirror. The dissatisfaction was gaining ground.

It was then that we — a somewhat uninterested man and his dissatisfied wife — began going to church on a Sunday, just once a month. During the first service, as an observer, I immediately knew that these people had it all wrong. 'There may not be a God,' I thought, 'but if there was, I would certainly know how to worship him better than this.' I knew, for it was imprinted upon my memory, that unless the priest wore a chasuble, a maniple and a girdle to tie the stole over his cassock, he wasn't properly dressed for the occasion. Without the elevation of the host in a particular manner and the sounding of the sanctus bell, it wasn't a proper service. In the absence of the correct intonation of the voice there could be no doubt that the priest was not correctly addressing God, who, in any case, wasn't there to listen. I might be an atheist disguised as an agnostic, but I certainly thought I knew more about how to play their games than the Christians who were there.

Nevertheless, our monthly hour of self-inflicted pain continued — such was my regard for George Griffiths — and then autumn came again.

2

The Challenge and The Change

We didn't hear them come through the letter-box, we just found them on the doormat. They were leaflets announcing a mission that was to come to the village. By now, I had trained myself to scan literature rapidly and to make an immediate assessment of what was before me. The instant, assertively stated conclusion seemed well suited to the lifestyle I was moulding around myself and these bits of paper were to be the subject of the scrutiny they deserved; that of a few seconds only. 'Soap coupons' was my conclusion, 'valueless and gaudy'. I didn't know what a mission was but certainly its literature left a lot to be desired. Our interest was negligible and we were not drawn by these scraps.

A few days later, as I lay under the car of the moment, working away at its transmission, I heard heavy footsteps coming up the drive. They were a sound that over the following months I was initially to detest and then to look forward to as little else. My view was of a large pair of shoes surmounted by trousers whose cuffs didn't quite cover the tops of the shoes. Above my field of vision it might have been a farmer, wearing, as was usual, his trousers at half-mast, and enquiringly I greeted the stranger, as I emerged from beneath my car for a better view. He said that his name was David and he'd come to talk about the mission. He looked good for an argument and I thought I would probably enjoy myself crossing swords with someone from the church, so David was invited into the house. To introduce his subject, he explained what the mission was: it didn't help us. Over a mug of coffee he then discussed the contents of the literature we had received and I made sure that he saw I remained unimpressed. It was at that moment that Elizabeth recalled questions she had had about an article in the church magazine. Why we had started to take the church magazine I shall never know. It seems that it was a penalty for going to church and it certainly didn't sit well alongside my student's half-price copy of *The Times* and an assortment of scientific literature that littered the house. To my surprise, Elizabeth had been reading the church magazine and had asked me about an article called 'Operation Philip'. It baffled her for it spoke of the enemy and the battle. 'Who was the enemy, what was the battle?' she had asked me and I certainly didn't know. Now David was being plied with the same questions, and though he seemed to know, his explanation didn't seem to impart any knowledge to me. Our conversation was however, abruptly terminated after David made a comment containing a hint that we might not be Christians.

'Listen, if you want to make remarks like that, you'd better go next door. That's where the atheists live: we're Christians in this house,' I said. Looking rather trodden-on, David left a few moments later. For my part, I didn't believe a word I had said, but that didn't matter — I had successfully dealt with a situation in which I might have been drawn into talking about religion at a level beyond the trivial.

That was not the end of the matter though, for we were to find that the first day of the eight-day mission was on a Sunday when there was a crèche and so we went to church. In going, I, as usual, took on the mantle of a detached, cynical observer. I hadn't known the trouble to which the organizers of the mission had gone to get the man who, they felt, God wanted to lead the mission: all I knew was that I didn't like him. At the appropriate moment, the missioner ascended the pulpit to preach his sermon. It was my first shock to discover that he spoke with the wrong accent: he came from Liverpool and I came from the south. To this southerner, Liverpool was the land of clogs, wet streets and unkempt youths tunelessly playing guitars and shouting. More was to follow. As he spoke, he smiled, and this completely destroyed the picture of a solemn occasion in a sanctified building. Worse than that, though, he told a joke and my indignation was only exceeded when, in his excitement, he waved his hands around. Harry Sutton was not for me and in my view was not for the church either.

At the end of the service we drove to Bury St Edmunds where our friends Martin and Madeleine now lived. They had just abandoned going to church and to me seemed safer for it, so I didn't hesitate to tell them what we had witnessed that morning. As we had driven to their house I had said to Elizabeth, 'I don't know what the church is coming to, employing a circus act like that. They must be getting desperately short of members.' Our friends got the full force of my feelings before we returned home that evening.

Waiting for us on the doormat on our return home was a letter from a couple we had recently met. It contained an invitation to supper at their home but the invitation was so worded that we were clearly meant to be at the mission beforehand. The invitation pleased me — a little more social intercourse in life would be a good thing and I had liked our potential hosts at our first meeting — but the thought of going to the mission brought no pleasure at all. Weighing up the situation it was eventually decided that it would be worthwhile putting up with a little more religion in order to pursue the social contact, so the invitation was accepted.

Reluctantly we went to the mission to discover that, that night a Christian film was to be shown. I didn't know what to expect and the name of the originator, Billy Graham, meant nothing to me. 'Souls in Conflict' seemed dreadful, consisting of a series of half-a-dozen people walking around with miserable looks on their faces until something mysterious happened and one after the other they assumed silly grins. The story-line was weak and incoherent, I decided, but my anger was aroused by the last character, an engineer, who went through the process as the other characters and succumbed: I despised him.

When the film was thankfully over and a short epilogue completed by the missioner, we moved quickly to our car, giving sociable nods to people on the left and right, to drive to our hosts' home for supper. Ian and Denny lived a few miles away so they were in their car, some other guests elsewhere in convoy and we in our car. In the privacy of the car Elizabeth asked innocently, 'What did you think of the film?'

'It was lousy,' I replied tartly.

'Now, Roy,' I was warned, 'Ian and Denny believe that sort of thing, so if they ask your opinion, don't be rude to them.' This conversation had gone on long enough and I terminated it with the blunt retort that would also remind my wife of what sort of stuff this objective scientist was made.

'If I think it's lousy, and I'm asked, I shall say it's lousy.'

We arrived at the attractive and comfortable home in silence. Introduced to the other guests, we made rather polite inconsequential conversation which brightened somewhat as the evening progressed. The flow of chat was, however, brought to an abrupt halt as Denny, our hostess, who was leading the conversation, picked me out from the group and asked, 'What did you think of the film?' It was a strange twist to the evening for we had successfully avoided talking about religious matters until this moment. Further, it seemed most unfortunate, that, while she could have picked on any of that small group of people, she would identify me. A straight question merited a straight answer and I would give it: I had to, for I had told Elizabeth exactly what I would do if asked about the film. It was a pity, for I had wanted to pursue the friendship with our hosts, but a vaguely defined quality which I called honour was at stake and honesty was to be my watchword.

'It was lousy,' I said. We left shortly afterwards, the evening having gained an uncomfortable chill in the shocked silence that followed.

It is, in retrospect, odd to record that I went to the next meeting of the mission on the following evening. There was no reason for this beyond the fact that Harry Sutton was due to speak to the Men's Society to which I went from time to time. There are moments though, when, as rationalistic as we order our lives to be, we behave in an irrational manner: this was one such moment. Yet in some way I wanted to lodge my protest against this man whom by now I despised even more than the character cast as an engineer in the film. To attack him verbally might not produce the desired result, for I would be arguing on his ground. That might be unsafe, and it would also break my general principle of not discussing religion. There had to be a more subtle way which gave him no opportunity to reply, but would offend and disturb him. Indeed there was, so I determined to arrive so late at the meeting that he, knowing how quickly one could cross the small village in which we lived, would realize that my lateness was intentional. The ploy went further: since he would be speaking when I arrived I would disturb him by slamming the door to the hall, walking heavy-footed across the building and scraping my chair as I sat down.

My arrival was one hour after the meeting began, but my plan rather misfired, for he was just completing his talk as I entered. Nevertheless I did my stuff as a question-time commenced. How I detested this speaker with the permanent smile on his face and how I longed to see him destroyed by a barrage of withering questions and comments that would quickly undermine his quite untenable position! But it didn't happen that way.

After some questions a point was put that, to my philosophical mind, was ridiculous: I hoped that at the hands of the missioner it would get the treatment it deserved. It did. A further question was more banal and very efficiently fielded: with some pleasure I noted the authority shown by one side of the debate — but it was the wrong side and in consequence I realized that my sympathies were also on the wrong side. It was most disturbing to discover that my affection was disposed towards the man who I identified as my antagonist and, as I followed the development of the discussion, my disturbance turned to alarm. Thus far I had judged the proceedings on intellectual grounds, but carefully watching this strange man who had no characteristic that drew me to him, my intellectual detachment was suddenly swamped by the clear and undeniable, yet unquantifiable, observation that he had something about him that I had never seen before in anybody. What it was I could not understand, although in some way I identified it with the Christianity of which he spoke. Then, in horror, the realization broke upon me that what he had, I wanted.

It seemed ridiculous. I had worked for everything I had obtained and the career that a few years before had seemed impossible was almost within my grasp. The world was soon to become my oyster, when anything I wanted would be within my purchasing power. Yet this man had something which, intuitively, I knew I could not buy. The anger and frustration at that thought was however lost in the certain and quite irrational knowledge that not only did I desire what he had, I also wanted it more than anything I had or was likely to obtain: he had something that gleamed with greater intensity and had more importance than life itself as I knew it.

The meeting concluded and I was approached by the man in the heavy shoes. David stood quizzically in front of me, made one or two polite comments, then asked my opinion of the meeting. My arguments had, I thought, been carefully worked out in advance: a few appropriately spaced clichés in which famous philosophers or politicians of an atheistic bent would be quoted would reduce David to silence. I pointed out to him that my arrival at the meeting had been late so I didn't really know what the missioner had spoken upon — yes, he had noticed my entry, so the first point was mine. Now, to move quickly to game, set and match, I began to display my wares, but the discussion didn't go in the way that I had decided. David seemed to have an answer to every point — my cut and thrust had no effect at all and my waspish comments about the opium of the masses left no mark. Soon I was to realize that it was not David, but I, who was reduced to silence.

David continued gently, but authoritatively, and as the minutes passed I knew that control of the conversation had slipped away from me and was in his hands. Looking about me after a while, I noticed that there were only the two of us remaining in the hall, and glancing at my watch I commented that is was getting rather late — perhaps we should draw the discussion to a close.

'Of course, but shall we have a prayer before we go?' invited this strange man. Pray? But that was quite impossible, for to begin with there was no priest present and I knew that people didn't pray unless led by a priest: apart from that I wouldn't know what to do. Looking at David, I realized that he was bigger than me and fleetingly I wondered if he was dangerous, so decided that the best thing to do was to humour him and agreed.

'Then let's sit down,' he continued. All semblance of my control of this meeting had disappeared but in a despairing attempt to regain some initiative I replied,

'I'd rather stand up if you don't mind.' This we did as David prayed and, to this day, I still don't know what he prayed about, so terrified was I.

★　　★　　★

We left the hall and for me it was like stepping into freedom. There were no street lamps in the village and on that night there appeared to be little by way of a moon. As we prepared to go in different directions I said idly, 'I'm sorry that we're so late: your family will be concerned about you.'

'It's all right,' he responded, 'I don't have a family, and I live in digs.'

'In that case you will have missed your supper,' I said. But that, too, didn't evoke any concern in him. Then, in the silence that followed I heard a voice say,

'Would you like to come home and have some cocoa with me?' David looked a little surprised, but that was nothing to my amazement as I realized that it was *my own* voice that I had heard.

In minutes, this man, of whom I was more than wary, was ensconced in my living room while I was, in some agitation, searching the kitchen shelves for a tin marked 'Cocoa' and then reading the instructions on how to make it. My wife was safely in bed and the resultant brew had little to commend it, but since I have never asked anyone to have cocoa with me before, we had to take whatever came — I knew no better. We sat and he talked. In fact, he talked until three o'clock in the morning and it was as if there was opening before me a casket of jewels. Two things shone beyond anything else. This man believed the Bible. I had never met anyone who had that view of the Bible: of course it was good literature, excellent poetry, interesting history, even an unique combination of mythology and folklore, but to countenance believing it was entirely novel.

We had a Bible in the house, hidden in a remote corner of the bookcase, but it certainly served no useful purpose beyond being, by its presence, an acknowledgement that literate people lived in the house. There was a further revelation, besides which the rather quaint belief in the contents of a book paled into insignificance: he didn't need to say it to me, but I recognized that as he spoke about a person called Jesus, David clearly knew him.

I was staggered yet had to concede that his points were convincingly put, not by eloquent argument but by being who he was. That, though, was not acceptable to me and at that point, in order to put matters back into the framework that I understood, I said to him, 'David, I'll accept your God on one condition only. If I can take a clean sheet of paper, placing on the top line a proposition that is entirely rational and proveable, developing the argument down the page as a mathematician would develop a proof, each line representing an entirely logical development of the former until I can write at the bottom line, "Therefore God exists — QED"; in that circumstance only will I accept your God.' It sounded good, for I was now talking in terms that to me were familiar.

'That you will never do,' David replied. But how could

he make that statement, for he knew nothing about intellectual techniques or philosophical analysis? At that he left and I, a worried yet determined man, slipped into bed for a few hours sleep before another day at my desk in the office I now had at the university of Cambridge.

★　　★　　★

With the new day there was a determination to carry through my claim: I would prove whether or not God existed. Certainly this could only be approached philosophically, but the same principles of integrity and reasoned development that one would use in a mathematical proof would also be valid here. If the investigation was to be on philosophical grounds, then what better place to deal with it than in Cambridge, this hot-bed of intellectualism. Surrounded as I was by a diversity of people united in one respect, intellectual achievement, I was sure that I had been transfused through four years or so by the atmosphere that seemed to pervade the corridors. I sat at my desk, moved all my papers to one side, and, blank sheet before me, sought in my mind for the reasonable premise upon which to develop my thoughts. Over four days many came: the world could not have been duped for two thousand years; the structure of our society could not have been based on a fallacy; the order of the cosmos could not be an accident. Arguments developed in my mind one after the other but always I seemed to reach an impenetrable barrier and four days after starting the exercise I had to admit that there had been no progress. Yet lofty as those thoughts were, I kept coming back to the infuriating observation — David knew Jesus.

Saturday evening came: I had kept away from the mission since Monday night, but now, because of a previously made agreement, Elizabeth promised to go to the meeting. It was a social evening; there would be tea and cakes and Elizabeth had been asked to help make the tea. She went and in due course I followed. Again my entry was late, not this time because of malicious intent, and as I slipped in to the meeting to sit alongside

Elizabeth, a lady called Pauline rose to give what was called a testimony. What was involved in a testimony I was yet to discover, but as it was revealed to me alongside the revelation of this lady's life, I was bemused. She was sharing personal matters that embarrassed me and the embarrassment was made the more acute by the fact that, at crucial moments within her life story, Jesus made an entrance and problems appeared to be resolved.

Pauline's story was followed by a hymn and, had I looked at Elizabeth, I would have noticed that she was weeping. She couldn't understand her reaction but thought, that because we were singing to a Welsh hymn tune, she was homesick: yet homesickness had never been part of the loneliness of her life. As the meeting concluded, the missioner invited anyone who wished to know more of Jesus Christ to ask him for the little red book at the door. Before we left the hall, though, David had mysteriously appeared at our side and was enquiring our opinion of the meeting. I had re-organized my arguments only slightly since the previous occasion and this time they had a somewhat worn feeling about them, making no more impact than before.

David returned to our house, yet it was not apparent why. Cocoa was again served, though this time it was made better, and our visitor probed away gently at us. The discussion passed between him and Elizabeth, while I sat in a rather sulky silence knowing that my armoury had been expended. Rather to my surprise, Elizabeth commented, 'When the missioner invited people to take the little red book at the door, I wanted to, but since no one else did, I didn't either.'

David replied, 'That was God speaking to you.'

'God speaking to me?' Elizabeth echoed, 'I know that he spoke to people in Bible days, but surely he doesn't do so now.'

There was a silence in which a sentence formed in Elizabeth's mind: 'Ask this man to pray for you.'

'Impossible,' she reasoned, 'I don't even know him,' so she broke the silence by saying, 'Anyway, I shall never be good enough to meet God.'

'You can meet him now,' was David's response, 'would you like to pray?'

My astonishment at being an observer of this curious conversation was heightened the more when my wife eagerly agreed, and, with the visitor to our house, bowed her head. They prayed and Elizabeth admitted that she was a sinner, stating that she believed Jesus to have died for her to become her Saviour and she asked him to come into her life, committing herself to him.

There are moments in life when our critical faculties are brought to bear in a concentrated way upon a situation, for we know that a lot depends upon the accuracy of our observation. The training I had had in experimental observation, developed from the first occasion I had seen an aero-engine run to the detailed research executed on cascades of aerofoils, had included watching engines disintegrate rapidly and also viewing the remains of a prototype airliner after a disastrous crash in which all the occupants were killed. The perception I had employed had led, in the scientific context, to reporting what was reckoned to be accurate, but at a personal level it had left indelible memories upon my life. Now there was the opportunity to use this developed faculty, viewing my wife as the subject of an experiment that went beyond the theoretical modelling I had attempted during the week. A lot depended on the observation about to be made.

Elizabeth and I had known each other for fourteen years and naturally I knew her very well: her attitudes, feelings and reactions were, by now, easily predicted. I knew her as I knew myself, although one or two events in the previous few days had me wondering how well I did know myself. She looked up from her prayer and I knew that the worst had happened: she was transformed. Her face shone as I'd never known it, tears channelled down her cheeks and her joy was clearly beyond restraint. All that she could do was to shake the stranger's hand and repeat, 'Oh, thank you, thank you.'

Now I had a problem. My smug, anti-religious arguments had been brushed aside, my wife was suddenly a person whom I'd never yet met and at the same time the philosophy of my life — a detached intellectualism that could not countenance the existence of God — was shattered. All that I could do in the circumstance was to try to change the course of events.

'Go and make some coffee, Elizabeth,' I ordered without realizing that I would, as a result, be left alone with the religious lunatic who was upsetting my life. In the moments that we waited for the coffee I became the focus of his attention, but I halted any further conversation by saying,

'David, you'll never get me on this emotional high-tide.'

Viewing me coolly, he replied, 'I realize that. You know, there's a verse in the Bible that says 'The harvest is past, the summer is ended, and we are not saved.' At that the coffee made an entry, I was careful to maintain a social chit-chat and, to my relief, David went home. We went to bed, Elizabeth with a look on her face reminiscent of that of the people I'd seen in the film almost a week before.

Sleep has rarely eluded me, but that night it did. The hours crept by, as in the darkness of a room not even lit by the moon, I moved from one position to another to avoid incipient cramp and find a more comfortable attitude in which to yield myself to sleep. My mind remained alert, though, as I grappled with the events of the week. Seven days before, everything was set for a well-oiled future and a career that was, at the least, very promising. In the passage of a few days and over one or two conversations the whole balance of life had been upset: nothing seemed certain any more. Where did one start to unravel what had been presented? If there was no God, what was all the fuss about anyway? If he did not exist, what on earth had happened, before my eyes, to my own wife? On the other hand, if he did exist, this was the greatest challenge to my integrity as a scientist, for the enquiring mind of which I was proud, had failed to discover him or anything about him. Further, if he existed, what was the status of my atheistic philosophy?

Of course, I could look back to my religious period with some pleasure in the event of his being, but then what part had that played in bringing me into contact with his reality? The unavoidable answer was 'none'. That being the case, of what value in his eyes had been the whole of that religious life? I was forced to conclude that, again, the answer was 'none'. It was tautological that if years of that religious exercise had produced no result when there was a result to be had, then those years were fruitless. Reaching out to what might be before me — and certainly what Elizabeth had — automatically meant discarding that part of my past as useless. Could I do that? To do so implied that not only was I wrong as an atheist, I had also been just as wrong as a religious man, for the result in both cases had been the same — no experience of God. To admit an error here or there shows in life that one is big enough to stand it, but to admit that the error was consistent through life and was total, was more than I felt I could face.

The reverie was disturbed by a most remarkable incident. Lying on my back in bed, looking ahead of myself at nothing in the darkness, I saw a large panoramic picture open up. It was of an English country scene: the background was of elm trees in front of which was a beech hedge surrounding a field which had been sown with wheat. But — of course — it was autumn and harvest! Perhaps all those autumns of my life had pointed forward, with their anticipation of something new, to this moment with a promise of something beyond my wildest dreams. I saw the trees in the dark green they assume just before going into the reds and browns of autumn, the beech hedge already brown and crisp and the field, which had recently stood proud with its wheat crop, shorn to a five-inch stubble. To my right the stubble took the eye to a fairly close horizon but the dominant feature of that view was of the strips of alternating browns, each about eight feet wide, left by the combine harvester, the remains of the stalks leaning slightly one way or the other. The straight lines marking the progress of the combine harvester impressed me and I thought that a good job had been done. My curious gaze moved to the left and about twenty feet in front of me I saw, on the other side of the field but not quite in its corner, a single stalk of wheat still carrying its head. The head was full, heavy and ripe and moved gently in a slight breeze. The path of the combine harvester had just missed it and I reflected upon its fate. The seed had been planted, it had germinated, grown, come to fruit and ripened but it was as good as dead already, for the wind would blow it down and the rain would rot the grains in the head. Further, no farmer would bother to get out his combine harvester to take in one head of wheat.

There is usually some definable form of reasoning that takes the mind from one matter to the next, but I was quite unable to recognize any in the next thought that came to me. In a startling moment I knew that the head of wheat on its stalk was me. The realization horrified me, but to underline in all its awfulness my situation, I heard an audible Voice speak in the silence of the room, 'The harvest is past, the summer is ended, and we are not saved.' Never before had I heard voices: that was for metaphysicians not scientists. Again, but louder, the words were spoken and repeated several times over with progressively increased volume. Finally, the Voice boomed four words over and over again, 'We are not saved, we are not saved, we are not saved.'

Reasoning and resistance evaporated in a moment as in terror I apprehended the fact that the God, of whom I was making philosophical propositions to demonstrate his non-existence, was speaking to me.

But what it was to be saved I didn't know and as I listened to words that I was much later to discover in the Bible at Jeremiah 8:20, I also contemplated the possibility that it might be too late for whatever being saved entailed. There needed to be no more convincing of the existence of God — he had spoken — but now my problem was even more fundamental: without his existence the question of salvation didn't occur, but now that his being was established beyond any doubt in my heart, how to be saved was of paramount concern. In not even knowing what the word meant I didn't know how to go about it, neither did I know to whom I could turn for advice.

★ ★ ★

Dawn came slowly and a new day brought new thoughts. It was time to get back to a reasoned way of living, but unfortunately things had changed and, in particular, Elizabeth was undeniably quite different. She went to church and I returned to my Sunday morning pastime of lying under the car to bolt up bits that were hanging off.

For Elizabeth her first steps as a new Christian included an unexpected challenge. An acquaintance called Margo met her in the village. Their talk drifted in the general direction of the church mission when Margo exclaimed, 'I really can't stand these Christians. All they do is walk around with silly grins on their faces.' Elizabeth was mortified at her friend's observation and, moreover, at the prospect of being identified with such people. Nevertheless, an hour or so later Elizabeth returned full of joy saying, 'Roy, you must go tonight: it really is wonderful. I hope you decide.'

The day wore on and the pressure became intense. Again my logical nature was under heavy attack and my wife was no help. Finally I succumbed to her request and, leaving her to look after the children, I went to the final service of the mission. The missioner was the same: cheerful, joking and generally acting in an entertaining way. As he finished his address he told a story that riveted me. It concerned two men who recited, before an audience, Psalm 23, one a Shakespearian actor who was eloquent, the other a humble peasant who was not. The latter though had the impact and the actor observed wryly, 'I know the words, he knows the author.' That was it: I had had a lifetime of learning words, my science, my reading, my Bible as a young man and the form of service which I could recite standing on my head — but I didn't know the author. It was as if the light of understanding was dawning as I concluded that I must, at all costs, know the author, but there was still a resistance, for within me I heard a voice say,

'You don't want to have anything to do with this,' and to my surprise, a second voice within replied,

'But they've got what you want.'

The first countered, 'Look at them, they're all country bumpkins.'

The second responded, 'But they've got what you want.'

The first, 'But you're not like them, you're an intellectual!'

The second, 'But they've got what you want.'

Then the first voice said, 'What would your friends at Cambridge University think if they knew you were mixed up in this?'

Nothing could have been more piercing, yet the second voice replied, 'But they've got what you *need*.' The variation of one word in the reply did it and my mind was made up: I would take a step and ask at the door for the little red book. I waited till most people had left the building since this was to be a private moment of which no one in the world would know. Every action was planned: I would approach the missioner, ask for the book and slip it immediately into a jacket pocket whose flap I slipped inside to smooth the fast process — then I would leave quickly.

It didn't happen that way, but I did ask for the little red book. The missioner looked delighted, putting on the by now familiar smile from the film — I believe I was his only customer that week — and he took from behind his back a vivid red folder about ten inches by fourteen inches. With horror I realized that it would never fit into my pocket, but I had to take it or someone would observe the transaction.

It is, of course, the correct thing to pray, confessing the problems of the past life, turning from them to Christ and asking him to become Saviour. I didn't do that: in fact I didn't do anything but take the book. In that instant the God who had patiently set the scene over the years, had pointed me towards engineering from an arts-orientated school, had taken me through academic institutes so that I could be in Hemingford Grey, had listened silently as I aired my intellectual objections to his existence and who had in sovereign majesty thundered his word at me, then filled my soul, my life, my all. I was yet to learn that I had been born again. Life would never be the same again, for it would be my discovery that everything had changed. My objectives in life, my family relationships, my attitude to my work, even my thought processes were to experience a total change, emanating in entirety from the one simple and undeniable fact that the new birth had in that moment become my experience.

3

Outreach and Infilling

It may have been meant to be a secret, but it didn't stay that way. From the record, it seems that Elizabeth and I were the only two who had made a response at the mission and this news was clearly filtering around. David immediately drew alongside us and offered to help guide us in the early days in any way he could. He came to our house for the evening and then the next and the next. It was evident that he had thrown his diary of engagements away as he began to nurture us and within a few days I was being encouraged to tell people what had happened. Surveying my range of friends the decision was made to tell George Griffiths on the following Sunday so, as a group of us walked from the church building to the church-room for the after service cup of coffee, I singled him out and said, 'George, I'd like you to know that last Sunday I became a Christian.' The secret was out. George stopped, turned towards me, his eyes full of tears and his face full of love.

'I know,' he replied, 'but I wanted to hear it from your mouth.'

George died a year or so later and I went to the memorial service. There I learned how this old man had arrived in the village and badgered the pastor until they began praying together and then continued to badger him for 'an aggressive evangelistic outreach based upon the church.' It was George who had been behind the scenes pushing away and after that memorial service, in conversation with a friend of his, I learned that it was

George who had been praying for Elizabeth and me consistently for two years before our conversions.

It was a couple of years after that we learned that George's hadn't been the only prayers of which I'd been the subject. At a Christian family conference in Hertfordshire I met a Miss Watkins who, it turned out, lived in Bristol, my long-vacated home town and nearly two hundred miles away. After general chat we discovered that we had both resided in Horfield; after further discussion that, for a period had lived in the same street — and then that we had been next-door neighbours.

In the excitement Miss Watkins said, 'You must have been the little curly-headed boy who played in the garden of the next house twenty-five years ago.' I assured her that this was so.

Miss Watkins then added, 'My mother and I used to sit in my bedroom window which overlooked your garden and, as we watched you play, we used to pray for you.' A quarter of a century later the results of her prayers were presented for her to see.

There were many things we were to learn of in the early days: that prayer is vital was one of them. Prayer in fact was the vehicle of all our early experiences of the Lord's working.

The three of us looked at one another, not really knowing what was now to happen. Elizabeth had been a Christian for about thirty-six hours yet I was a mere day old in this new life. David realized that he had a problem: he'd never had new Christians on his hands before, although from where we stood, he seemed like an assured professional, unflappable. Enthusiastically I had declared that our discovery was of prime importance and something should be done about it, but what? With some hesitation David mentioned that the pastor of the church had it in mind to start Bible studies around the village and if we would care to be involved perhaps we could have one in our own home. That was excellent, but I realized that we had a problem: neither Elizabeth or I knew one end of the Bible from the other. David confided that he had been a Christian for eleven years and had read the Bible right through at least once so, with such a qualification, he was immediately acclaimed as our mentor.

'Now,' I said, 'who do we ask? What about . . .?' and a list of names came easily to mind.

'Roy, you don't do it that way,' volunteered our new teacher, 'you pray and ask God to bring along those he wants.' The instruction sounded crazy, but I recalled that he had been correct about salvation and that had sounded pretty crazy too, so we decided to try it.

We began to pray and, in a week, something wonderful occurred. Margo, who was also a mother of young children, had met Elizabeth and something of a casual friendship had grown. It was Margo whom Elizabeth had met when a few hours old in her new-found Christian faith and had made the observation about the 'silly smiles on their faces.' A day before I could have agreed warmly with her perception, yet this rather unpromising introduction to the subject had led to the news that we were to have a Bible study in our home. Margo immediately became our first candidate. Kenneth was a bank-clerk in Cambridge and we had adopted an informal ride-sharing arrangement when I found myself, rather reluctantly, sharing with him that I embraced a Christian interest. His response was warm and he became our second candidate. Number three was a farmer's wife who had heard about the Bible studies and wanted to come. We had neighbours across the street, Mark and Mavis with whom we were acquainted. Mark's mother owned a small-holding with chickens so they were a source of cheap eggs, a dozen of which we purchased weekly. While Mavis seemed human, Mark's character was that of an ogre. He had a short, abrasive temper and had the frequent habit of airing it. We probably wouldn't have continued to buy the eggs except that they were cheap and we were very poor, so weekly we ran the gauntlet of his displeasure. To ease the unpleasantness, Elizabeth and I took it in turns to fetch the eggs and regularly each was sure that it was the other's turn. Mavis met Elizabeth one day and, commenting upon the mission of the week before, said that there was a lot she didn't understand and many questions she had to ask. Elizabeth hesitatingly mentioned the proposed Bible study and Mavis became our fourth victim. All looked fine until a day later, a knock on the door announced Mavis' presence. Yes, she was looking forward to coming to the meetings, but could she bring somebody with her?

'Of course,' we replied, 'anybody you like. Who are you bringing?'

'Mark,' was the chilling reply.

It was, then, a motley group that gathered at eight o'clock on Thursday evening. We all felt uncomfortable since none of us knew what was even involved in a Bible study and as we eyed one another, my most fearful looks were reserved for Mark who, I knew, ran on a short fuse and could go 'pop' at any moment. A short prayer and we were off.

David said, 'I think we will begin by reading John 1:1, "In the beginning was the Word, and the Word was with God, and the Word was God."' What sort of conundrum was that? In minutes there was involved conversation, David by turn, standing back, guiding, plucking a scripture from nowhere; a quick cup of coffee so that time would not be wasted, a return to prayer and then back to John 1:1. Suddenly, it was after midnight and everyone left, promising to be back next Thursday. How we had kept interest going for so long we couldn't assess, but we were later to learn that a midnight finish was the mark of a short meeting. As the interest deepened in our lives it was quite normal for the study to go until at two or three o'clock and sometimes, at four o'clock in the morning, the last straggler would be creeping down the drive for a hasty hour or so in bed before beginning the new day's work. The pattern was always the same — John 1:1, prayer and discussion forming the content and occasional cups of coffee to lubricate our throats. In the several months that those meetings ran we never got beyond John 1:2 as the basis for study.

It was through that period I learned a valuable principle in prayer. The Bible studies covered the time when I was finishing at Cambridge and beginning a new job in Derby. It was a busy time and when I commenced the work with Rolls-Royce my family was still in Hemingford Grey, necessitating the frequent trip of almost a hundred miles each way. Three or even four hours sleep a night was not compatible with the exertions of the day, but six or eight were, so I began to pray that for every hour's sleep the Lord would grant two hours rest. Prayer worked for an objective scientist as I thus continued in physical freshness. There was just one occasion when the prayer didn't work and it came as a clear sign to me that I simply wasn't observing the effect of a physiological change in my body: it was also a sign that the Lord expects us to abuse neither the life he has given us nor the facility of prayer. The Vintage Sports Car Club, of which I had been an enthusiastic member, was meeting at a pub just outside Derby and I went to it to keep in touch with those things that I had for years enjoyed. Strangely, the hearty talk went over my head and the involved discussion about cars bored me. Feeling a little downcast I returned to my bedroom in Derby and, glancing at my watch, saw I had about four hours available for sleep before a busy day at the office. 'Two hours of rest for every hour of sleep, please Lord,' I muttered into the bed-covers and that's about as far as the prayer went. The next day I felt impossibly tired — and I fell asleep at my desk!

Meanwhile, David was still visiting us every evening, discussing both the Bible studies and our hang-ups. The Christian life was, for me, less than a week old when I assured David that my scientific principles were not to be scuppered.

'I reserve the right,' I said, 'to review the available data for the Christian case at regular intervals in a scientific fashion, and should I find new evidence to suggest that my decision to become a Christian is wrong, I shall cease to be one until there is more supporting evidence to convince me of the Christian claim.' David took on, what was to become a characteristic pose — knees slightly bent, right hand clutched to forehead and body leaning back a little — as he laughed, groaned and then looked appealingly to heaven.

'You don't do it that way,' he said, and had to say often, 'that's not a walk of faith.'

Of course, the Bible studies and people's reactions were a focus for the talks between the three of us and, at David's suggestion, we began praying in a personal way for the others in the group. Every week we would single one out for prayer, asking the Lord to call that one to himself. To our utter amazement, after the first week of prayer, the candidate for our intercession was born again. From then on, we had no doubts and as we prayed, they fell. Our Christianity was so guileless that we hadn't yet learned any of the standard teachings, including that principle that we mustn't expect conversions: we simply believed and the God, who week by week, planted the name in our hearts, drew the owner of the name to himself.

Mavis wasn't the first, but hers was one of the most startling of the conversions experienced. The evening had progressed and John 1:1 had again yielded fruit as Mavis came under a deep conviction. She recognized her need, especially in seeing that converted people around her who she knew, had been changed. Finally she asked for prayer and David led her in a word of commitment towards her conversion. We, sitting around the room, watched intently after the prayer for the emergence of the 'silly grin'. Instead though, Mavis looked up slowly and her eyes focused over and beyond my right shoulder. A look of wonder and sweet joy crossed her face and, in the silence, she whispered,

'I can see Jesus. He's standing in the corner looking at me.' It was a holy moment.

Mark, the abrasive husband of Mavis, remained abrasive. He never went 'pop' but there were some close-run moments. A week or so later he became the subject of prayer and with anticipation we waited for Thursday night to see how the Lord would do it. The evening

progressed and Mark seemed scarcely any different. As
three o'clock approached everyone, including Mark, went
home leaving David, Elizabeth and me looking at one
another in bewilderment. What had gone wrong? He
hadn't been converted — and certainly he should have
been. We had been analysing this unexpected lack-of-
event for almost half an hour, when the still of the night
was broken by a tapping at the front door. We didn't
normally have visitors at 3.30 a.m. so it was with curiosity
I opened the door to see an ashen-faced Mark looking
very forlorn, asking if he could have a private talk. He
came into our welcome arms and in moments had the
assurance of a new life, as he prayed his way to the
Saviour.

With one exception, everyone in the group had been
converted within about six weeks of the start of the Bible
study. Our hearts were heavy as that one who we had
seen coming under conviction, even airing needs, but at
the moment of yielding, had turned away. From that
moment we saw interest rapidly fade as it was evident
that the voice of the Lord was becoming fainter to that
ear. In three weeks the lady had left.

Now we were all Christians what should we do? I wanted to rush off and wheel in another bunch from the
village but David's counsel prevailed: we would stay, as a
group to study the Bible. So we continued with John 1:1.

We must have been looking at one of the remoter
parts of John 1:1 a couple of weeks later, when Margo
made an innocent and bright comment, 'You know,
David, that in the Bible it speaks of people talking in
tongues.'

'Yes,' came the reply in unexpectedly guarded tones
from David.

'There are churches where that still happens today,
aren't there?' rejoined Margo.

David coloured slightly and, with a hint of irritation in
his voice, said, 'I believe so. Let's get back to John 1:1
. . .'

As an aside in the mainstream of the evening's conversation I suppose it would have been lost except for

one thing. Two o'clock arrived and as usual, David was
the last to leave.

The three of us stood in the very small hallway and as
he moved toward the front door, Elizabeth said to David,
'You recall what Margo said about churches where
people speak in tongues.' Again there was that unexpected guardedness in David's voice as if he was waiting
to be trapped. Cautiously he agreed that he did recall
Margo's comment.

'You speak in tongues, don't you?' went on Elizabeth.

David turned bright red and blurted out, 'How on
earth do you know?'

'The Lord told me when Margo was talking,' replied
Elizabeth sweetly.

'What is this all about?' I demanded. 'What is "talking
in tongues"? This conversation is a mystery to me. David,
what's it all about?'

'I know nothing about it,' was David's hasty and very
uncomfortable rejoinder.

'Come along David, it's clear that you do. If this is
something from God, I want to know about it.'

Reluctantly David returned to the sitting room, more
coffee was prepared and he told us all he knew.

He had gone to a travelling evangelistic mission for
several nights, a month or so before, and to his surprise
had been convicted of the need to be baptized. This didn't
follow his denominational teaching but so convinced was
he, that having gone away on holiday, he had driven back
a hundred fifty miles for a baptismal service he knew
was to take place. The act of obedience completed, he
returned after putting on dry clothes to the meeting, to
hear an invitation for those who wanted to be baptized
in the Holy Spirit to go forward for prayer. He related
how in that moment he had felt a call from God just as at
his conversion eleven years before, so he responded.
Knowing nothing about it, he was told that, following
prayer, he would speak in new tongues, so he did. The
only advice he had was that the Lord would show the
next step. He continued, we learned, to speak thus in his
quiet time and, in particular, as he drove to the Bible

studies in Hemingford Grey. To his considerable astonishment he found that after eleven years in which he
had longed, but never managed to lead anyone to the
Lord, Elizabeth had immediately been born again. Within a day I had become a Christian and now there were
Margo, Kenneth, Mavis and Mark.

My scientific mind reeled: firstly, there was a God and
then he was a communicating God, then there was a new
and spiritual dimension to life and the knowledge of
salvation. All of these had been propositions of enormous magnitude to one whose esoteric engineering interests were, by comparison, positively mundane. But
now people could talk in languages that they had never
learned which I could be led to believe might even be
the communicating media of angels! This seemed too
much and, in any case, for what purpose? Mad as it all
seemed, the pragmatic scientist was able to draw a clear
conclusion. For eleven years David had longed to lead
people to the Lord and, when he didn't engage in this
curious activity of speaking in tongues, he had been unsuccessful. Now, in his quiet time — how quiet? — and
even in the car, he practised this phenomenon and the
unconverted were falling like ninepins.

By now I was working in Derby, so that on Fridays I
rushed home to Hemingford Grey for the news and
managed to last most of the weekend without sleep until,
on Monday morning, I drove through the dawn back to
my office. All other information came via a sporadic
series of frenetic telephone calls. 'Today's word from
the Lord . . . conviction of the need to be baptized . . . a
group going to a church elsewhere in the East Anglian
Fenland . . . baptized in the Holy Spirit . . . Elizabeth
speaking in tongues!' Elizabeth speaking in tongues!
What on earth was going wrong as soon as I was away
from the home for a few days?

Carefully, it was explained to me that members of our
group had felt the Lord speaking to them of the need to

be baptized. Discussion with the pastor gained a sympathetic ear and an admission that he couldn't do anything about it, so with his blessing a small group had gone to a church where it was believed there would be a baptismal service. There wasn't even a baptistry but the speaker had invited people to step forward for prayer. Elizabeth, wanting more of Jesus, chose to respond, following Denny our socialite friend at whose home we had had the disastrous supper. Elizabeth had heard Denny begin to speak in a new language and immediately so did Elizabeth. This really was too much: if David wanted to wear big shoes, trousers at half mast and speak in tongues, that was his business, but when my wife got up to antics I couldn't understand, the limit had been reached. My words of caution to her and my objections meant nothing.

A week or so later there was a signal event in the life of the Bible study and I wasn't there to witness it. As the group prayed, Elizabeth prayed in a language no one understood. Prayer continued after a short and somewhat embarrassed silence and, as people looked up, all eyes turned to David. What had happened, for nothing of this sort was in the stated rules? David turned to the Bible and after fumbling around for a while discovered a passage in 1 Corinthians that seemed to suggest this was the gift of tongues. 'But, it says here,' he added, 'that if this happens there should be an interpretation.'

'I don't know if it has anything to do with it,' said Mavis, 'but when Elizabeth spoke in that language I had some words in English come into my mind. Could that be an interpretation?' David didn't know but suggested that if it ever happened again and a person had some English words, they should speak them out and we would discover if it was an interpretation.

Of course, it did happen and Mavis spoke her words in English while Elizabeth spoke in tongues. The result was a cacophony — and not marked by any signs of success.

More searching followed and David read, 'Let all things be done decently and in order,' so he suggested that the English might follow the tongue, then we could hear it. So, the Lord led us into that remarkable aspect of the Christian relationship where, by his Holy Spirit he spoke to our hearts. And what words: we handled them as pure gold, discussing them afterwards and recognizing that the Lord God had spoken to us. Yet how sad it was, as the days passed into years, that such 'gifts' were taken as a sign that we were in a Holy Ghost-inspired meeting, but we never paused to consider what he was saying. That he had spoken had become enough, its own justification of where we stood.

The life of surprises had only just begun though and one night David interpreted, but no one had spoken in tongues — so we discovered prophecy. We had had no teaching, read no books, and weren't even aware that anyone else had the same experience, as we asked the Lord to lead us. At least, no one could accuse us of being brainwashed or subject to wrong teaching: there just wasn't any.

★   ★   ★

Through all this I was a bystander. I saw my wife leaping ahead in her spiritual life and those who had come to the Lord after me evidently leaving me in their wake as I wrestled with the problems of the unreasonableness of all I was seeing. By now the whole group was flowing in an exciting dimension of the Holy Spirit's activity, but stoically I was refusing to be moved. My Bible became chaff-like in its reading, I couldn't pray by myself and it was only the infrequent moment of elation that disturbed an increasingly miserable existence. I was asked to undertake two Christian duties in the village: to talk to the Youth Club about my experience of the Lord Jesus and separately, to be one of several people recording short testimonies on tape for later playing.

The visit to the Youth Club was going to be simple. I was articulate and had, in the mêlée of informed scientific circles, discovered that I was able to express myself with ease. The message for the youth of the village may be different, but the technique would be the same: in any case, they constituted a very uncritical audience. I rose to speak, completed a well-ordered first sentence, then froze. My mind was a blank; no word, no inspiration, just clammy hands. Rallying myself, I stumbled on to a hasty conclusion, conscious that the Christian cause in that youth club, carefully nurtured over many years, had suffered a grievous setback.

The recording would, however, be much more relaxed and I knew that I could cope with it. There would be no enquiring, anxious or even uninterested faces in front of me: I could marshal my thoughts in a well-conceived order, presenting them without pressure but with a calm conviction. As disasters go, this event deserved a red alert. The other candidates told their stories in simple terms and each carried a beautiful ring of truth. My turn came and I knew that my testimony would be used to appeal to the sophisticated elements of the audience, those who would be swayed by compelling reason. The phrases tumbled out in a series of randomly disposed and unrelated remarks, sentences lost their verbs and some of them their full stops. After a few moments of agony I retired from the microphone in confusion, humiliation and not a little sweat. The untrained housewives had given perfectly good reports, but the recording that needed vicious editing before it made sense was that of the man with the mind trained for intellectual order.

I was a worried man and it was beginning to dawn on me that whatever equipping I had for life at large and scientific endeavour in particular, I was ill-equipped for what I now wanted to do more than almost anything: tell others of Christ.

★ ★ ★

We moved house to Derby, but our immediate desire was to return to Hemingford Grey, particularly as the following weekend there was a meeting at the home of Ian and Denny when there was a visiting speaker. The plans to go were thwarted by a mysterious illness which laid me low: I couldn't even crawl out of bed without feelings of giddiness and nausea. Elizabeth, surveying me, decided to take matters in hand.

'Roy,' she said, 'I'm going to pray for your healing.' We had, by now, some evidence of physical healing in the village, but as usual, my scepticism tended to make me view such events in terms of statistical probability. Nevertheless, I felt so ill that I was willing to try anything. Elizabeth prayed. I felt embarrassed and no better.

After watching me anxiously for a minute or so, she said, 'You'd better get up, Roy.'

'Impossible,' I said, 'I feel too ill.' Her entreaties won the day though, and, certain that I would feel ten times worse, were that possible, I put my feet to the floor. The giddiness receded somewhat, so I set aside the bed-clothes and with them the nausea also left. I stood and within ten minutes was washed, dressed and sat in the car, feeling well.

We drove back to Huntingdonshire and the village of Hemingford Grey, and although I knew nothing about the prospective meeting beyond its location and time, I was sure that this was to be the day. All through the journey, the rational mind argued vehemently with the incontrovertible facts. I had no power or ability in my Christian witness, but so that I would have, the Lord was that day going to call upon me to resign my tongue, which was to me at that time the last bastion of my ownership. Such resignation would, I sensed, once more lead me into the regions of the unknown. Hadn't that step into the unknown at the time of my conversion been enough, or was life now to consist of one fearful step after another into uncharted areas? I wasn't to know that the only answer to that question could be 'Yes'. Yet if this was to be the pattern of life, what was to happen to the structure of my thought processes, my career, my whole life, all of which were built upon the concept that future progress in any domain was built on the basis of progress made thus far?

The battle raged in my mind as we arrived at the

meeting. The speaker brought no comfort to me: I wasn't being bidden by a thoughtful, sensitive, philosophical argument; I was being berated by a bully with hands the size of meat-plates waving on the ends of telescopic arms that thrashed the air with unpredictable sweeps. Again and again within my heart I reasoned with the Lord that it was quite unnecessary to be filled with the Holy Spirit, but I knew no response other than that this was the day.

'Give me a sign, Lord,' I pleaded; something that would leave no doubt in my disorientated mind.

The room in which we met had a curious architectural feature; a small window set high on the wall on either side of the fireplace and looking nowhere except at the eaves of the next house. Taking my eyes from the speaker, I glanced idly through one of the windows. As I did so, I caught sight of a white dove flying past. Thunderstruck, I asked the Lord if this could possibly be him speaking to me, then a second dove landed on the eaves so that I had a good long look at it.

'Let's bow our heads in prayer.'

The speaker's voice penetrated my battered thoughts, 'A person here with arthritis and we will pray for them . .'

My head was bowed, my eyes closed, yet I knew his passage across the room, I knew the moment his hand was laid on the candidate and I knew that, as resistance crumbled, the almighty God had also put his hand on my life, for violently I began to vibrate as I was filled with the clear sense of the presence of the awesome Lord of all.

In moments, with two other people, I was being escorted into a bedroom and a woman came to pray for us. This had to be the ultimate humiliation to a confessedly chauvinistic scientist, but there was no way out, and the three of us bowed in prayer. Now the defences were down and all I wanted was whatever the Lord wanted for me. The agony of the moment was interrupted firstly by the feeling of a lump rising in my being, but that was forgotten as, in the distance, I heard a voice burst forth in tongues. It was a torrent that grew in intensity as my ears focused on the source. I rejoiced in my heart that the Lord had touched someone in the room — and with such a clear anointing — but how I longed that it might have been me. Who was it though? Margo's voice was a good octave and a half higher than that I heard: perhaps it was Kenneth, yet the mighty effusion didn't come from his direction. With a slowly dissolving disbelief I was brought to the astonishing realization that the voice was mine. The fact broke in on me and I walked in heaven: nothing in my life had ever approached this moment as time and eternity seemed to blend: for this I had been made, called and chosen — I was walking with the Lord God.

My hands were grasped and placed on Kenneth and someone ordered me to pray for him. I just carried on. Apparently Kenneth was immediately filled with the Holy Spirit, speaking in tongues according to the Scriptures, but I wouldn't have heard him. Kenneth escaped my hands, looking like a bear-mauled individual and with Margo, who had also been filled, they left me alone in the room. Time ceased for me, yet some while later I discovered that my wife was kneeling by me. I returned to earth slowly, learning that tea had been consumed but there might be something set aside for me. Bashfully, we returned to the group of people below, making polite conversation, while in my mind I continued to try to grasp what had happened.

Could such a thing ever happen again, or was this a once-in-a-lifetime encounter with the living God? I excused myself, asking for the washroom. Locking the door behind me, I stood in the tiny cubicle, raised both hands to heaven, 'Now, my God, now,' I called. The room was transformed as, again, a torrent of language flowed from me and I stood in the glory of the incorruptible God. He was after all, unchanging.

4

Healing and Heartache

The new-born baby in the next street had pneumonia at birth, we learned. It was one of the features of living in a small village that news moved fairly quickly and although I didn't comprehend much that this news implied I did understand the chilling prognosis. The first three weeks of life had been spent in an oxygen tent, but now there was a 50% chance only of living. The natural sympathy that any parent would have for another in this type of situation seemed to be heightened as we discussed it and, not realizing the implications, we felt we would pray for the baby. We did, but we didn't know what to say, since we had no idea if the Lord was interested in this type of problem.

My own prayer went along the lines: 'Lord, we've had the opportunity to live on this earth, so it doesn't seem fair that this child may not enjoy the same chance. I don't know if there's anything you can do about it, but if it's your will perhaps you'll do something.' It wasn't much by way of a doctrinal statement and even less when regarded as an example of the prayer of faith, but I knew no better and we were all at about the same position. Prayer continued though and in three weeks we learned that the child was discharged from hospital in perfectly normal health. I determined that that was quite a remarkable coincidence.

The coincidence continued, however. It was a couple of weeks after that surprising result that we learned of the desperate situation of a twenty-seven-year-old woman from the other side of the village. She had just given birth to her second child but extreme post-natal pain had led to the discovery that there had been congenital fault in the mother's spine; a full complement of vertebrae, but no discs to separate them. Strong back muscles had thus far through her life supported the spinal column, so that the problem had remained undetected, but the strain of bringing forth a child had telescoped the spine with the resultant trapping of many nerves. Doctors were alarmed, declaring that they knew of no medical precedent and the only recommendation that they could make was that she would spend the remainder of her life lying on a bed, so that the spine would at least be horizontal.

As an engineer, my own solution would have been to fit nylon bushes, but that maybe is why I never went into the field of medicine. The group discussed this news and found themselves praying for her. Prayer was not yet particularly familiar ground to us, but this sort of prayer was distinctly strange. To me it represented a point where my spiritual life, in which nothing was really tangible, would meet my scientific life of observation where that which is not quantifiable in measurement didn't really exist. While my interest was heightened as a result, I felt very uncomfortable about it all: the life of science was concerned with proving what is, so if nothing happened as a consequence of the prayer, what proof was there to support the very fragile Christian life that, as yet, I had? Better perhaps not to pray at all, turning a blind eye to the possible consequences of no answer than to risk losing everything in a resurgence of doubt and agnosticism. At least a 'no-answer' situation would remain hypothetical. At the same time, the evidence that prayer for the sick was likely to be answered was pretty flimsy: a three-week-old child had recovered from pneumonia — statistically insignificant — and I had in any case already credited it as a coincidence.

The lines along which I prayed were vaguely, 'Lord, this woman has a problem for which medicine has no solution. I don't know if there's anything that you can do about it, but the child did seem to get better when we prayed. Could you do something about this, please?'

Over the following weeks there was a progression of reports via a friend of the invalid. The first that we heard was that she was being permitted to move a little. About a week later the news was that she had been allowed to sit up in bed and this was followed shortly afterwards with the information that she could now sit in a chair. Within a couple of weeks we were told that she was walking and, six weeks after we began praying for her, she was discharged from hospital, being told by the perplexed staff, 'We can find nothing wrong with you.'

For me, the spiritually discernible and the physically quantifiable had met and I was persuaded that we had found something of monumental importance. Further, my statistical sample had doubled.

My weekly round, Monday to Friday at work in Derby and Friday to Monday at home in. Hemingford Grey, had begun. The weekends were times when I stuffed myself with spiritual food for support during the week when, slowly, it all seemed to drain away. It was a saw-tooth sort of existence with well-defined spiritual highs and lows. To help me over this period I was recommended to make contact with the pastor of a church in Derby where it was known there was a midweek prayer meeting and Bible-study.

On the appropriate night I arrived at the correct address in the city centre. My Christian life had been lived, in its entirety, in the surroundings of a small, but lovely, medieval building on the bank of a placid river running into the Fens. The tranquillity and the beauty perfectly complemented each other. My pre-Christian religious life had also known beautiful surroundings: for years a superb Georgian building had been the centre of activity, its complex ornaments standing in a remarkable harmony with the unique multi-domed ceiling, at the mathematics of whose curves I had often marvelled. Later, I

had been part of the congregation meeting in an out-
standing Gothic creation, reckoned by many to represent
the ultimate in architectural expression in that transitional
period between Decorated and Perpendicular Gothic
styles. But all of that was in the past, for as I stood in
Derby outside the place given on my piece of paper, I
was filled with horror. Before me was a monstrous and
dirty Victorian edifice built as a music-hall, but which
had evidently fallen on bad times. The traffic roared by,
depositing yet more dirt on its haggard façade and it
seemed to be in terminal illness. I later learned that its
original music-hall splendour had been exchanged for
the trappings of a political club, before the final indignity
of housing a church.

Worse was to come. The front door was locked, so I
found my way down some steps to the basement, carefully avoiding the numerous rubbish bins but still trip-
ping over abandoned refuse, before locating another
door. The large room into which I entered was a revelation: the walls were covered by a series of mirrors made
up of thousands of little rectangular mirrors to give the
viewer a fragmented image of himself. These were interspersed with gaudy travel posters recommending that I
should go to Italy, the Mediterranean, Greece — anywhere would have done for me at that moment. The
picture presented by the naked bulb on the flex des-
cending from the ceiling seemed to be a cross between a
1940s dance-hall and a travel agency.

Escape seemed desirable, but it was already too late
for I had been spied by the man who, I was to find, was
the pastor. He didn't look the part: winkle-picker shoes
were surmounted by a blue suit which was itself too light,
the lapels and jacket were too long and the whole was
crowned with a haircut consisting of curls on top and a
curious treatment to the sides and back, which gloried
under the name of D.A. As he approached me, everything inside me recoiled, but as he extended his hand
towards me and said, 'God bless you — welcome,' I knew
that I'd arrived at home.

The prayer meetings were marvellous. They were

held in a fairly small room that actually exceeded the
mirrored hall in vulgarity. This room was full of doors
and every one had been painted in a different paint,
primary and secondary colours jostling one another. It
was a good job that my tradition demanded that my eyes
should be closed whilst in prayer. An asthmatic gas fire
wheezed continually and perhaps ought to have been
the subject of intercession, but there were other things
to be about. I was impressed with the prayer-life around
me: there was a vibrancy, a directness and a joy that was
new to me. Further, I had to acknowledge that these
folk, with whom in the natural I seemed to have little in
common, prayed with a fluency for which I longed.

It was shortly after beginning the regular Wednesday
evening descent past the rubbish bins that, one evening,
we learned that Beryl was to be the subject of prayer.
Beryl, I discovered, was a nursing sister in a local hospital and she needed prayer for breast cancer. Now, to
me, this was an intriguing situation: this woman was
prepared to approach the Lord God in a matter with
which she was professionally familiar and to which she
could bring a professional eye to assess the result. What
was more, maybe her life and certainly her health was at
stake. Forty or so people were crammed into the room as
one or two laid hands upon her and we all prayed. The
air was stifling, everyone was breathing, every body was,
as always, giving off heat and the gas fire was adding its
own heat and sound to the chorus. Suddenly, I felt a
cool, constant draught blowing across the back of my
right hand and thought that it was a pity that someone
should open a door at that moment. Glancing up, I saw
that no door had been opened and then recalled that
somewhere in the Bible I had read about the wind of the
Spirit. Had it been my privilege to sense that divine
breeze?

A week later we had a report back from Beryl. Daily
she had felt the lump reduce in size until on the morning of the operation it was the size of 'a small pea, half
the size of the small fingernail' as she put it. Her explanation to the surgeon at the hospital that she had been

healed was gently set aside by the specialist, who said that he would like to make an incision to check it.

'Of course, I might discern that you are healed, but if there is any malignancy I shall operate immediately,' he said with authority.

With that agreement the exploration was undertaken and the surgeon finally made the declaration: 'I can find no lump and no malignancy.'

The news stayed fresh with me as I took it back to Hemingford Grey, repeating the action, blow by blow. My conviction that the Lord was able and willing to bring physical healing was now beyond reasonable doubt: I had seen prayer on three occasions for different and serious conditions and the results were indisputable. How the physics of the healing took place I didn't know, but I could not deny this impressive evidence.

My belief in the effectiveness of the prayer for healing was soon to be demonstrated in an unusual way. Home from Derby for the weekend, I caught influenza. The normal run of the ailment meant that I would be home for three to four days and would thus miss being at the office. At the same time I would have the chance to see a little more of my family whom I was missing.

David's visits were continuing and so it was to a sick house he came that weekend. After a few minutes he suggested that we might pray that I would be healed.

'No,' I replied quite sharply, 'I think that I would appreciate a few days at home. If you pray for me I'll have to be off to Derby again early on Monday morning.'

David didn't pray but later confided to Elizabeth, 'I think that Roy didn't want me to pray for him because his faith that he would be healed was certainly greater than mine.' I thus lay at home, suffering for a few days and thoroughly enjoying myself.

★   ★   ★

Our ignorance over those early days could hardly have been greater: we knew nothing about the Bible and, at a later date, David, to whom we looked at all times for leadership and advice, said he was never more than five minutes ahead of any of us. If anything could have gone wrong, it certainly should have done so with us. We were to learn that the Lord God was able to keep us from falling and, at the same time, also lead us into all truth. As an event would occur which opened our eyes and astonished our hearts, we discovered that within a day we would find authentication in our Bible reading. Ours was not an experience in which we read the Bible as an instruction book to which we had to conform for the Christian life to be manifested. We lived the experience, then found the confirmation in the Bible which we discovered to be a lamp unto our feet and a light to our path. One vivid example occurred as the Lord began to make us aware of his healing ability.

The Festival of Light, a major gathering, was scheduled to take place in London and, with many thousands of Christians, we made our way to Trafalgar Square for the great day. Arriving early in the morning we met a friend who mentioned the name of a man of whom I had often heard, but never met. He was just a few yards away, we were told and an introduction could be made. Eagerly we accepted and in moments were talking to the man. Elizabeth, seeing some friends, slipped away to greet them and, a few minutes later I too, turned to follow her. Whilst talking to the newly-introduced friend I had noticed that we were being closely watched by a couple from a distance of four or five yards. As I stepped away from my conversation, the lady of the couple darted forward and caught my arm.

'Are you . . .?' she asked, mentioning the name of a well-known Christian with whom I had no noticeable resemblance whatsoever.

Sounding slightly startled I said that I wasn't, but she countered, 'Well, you are one of those people who speaks at conferences, aren't you?'

Anxious not to be drawn into anything, I assured her that I certainly was not but, with a hint of desperation in her voice, she added, 'But can't you say something to my friend? You see he was sent home from hospital this week to die.' I looked at the object of her concern, a black man from, I guessed, central Africa, his face heavily lined through pain and grief.

She was evidently a friend, many years younger and she continued, 'It's not that he's worried that he is dying of cancer, it's the thought of leaving his children behind him. I say to him that he doesn't have to worry about that,' and now she waved her arm expansively around the growing crowd in Trafalgar Square, 'for there is the whole of this large family to look after them.'

What could I say to a man whom I had never met before, who was standing in pain, had been told that he was soon going to die and was in torment over the fate of his children? How I started the conversation is hard to recall but as we talked, he told me of his life, his conversion, then his falling away from God, adding that the cancer was the Lord's judgement upon him. With this I certainly did not agree, telling him that there was a day of judgement, but that was for the future: this was the acceptable year of the Lord. He went on to tell me that the cancer had been contracted some years before, but that he was prayed for by a man for whom he had a great respect and he had been healed.

The man before me continued, 'He was always greatly used in prophecy and his prophecies always came true. One day though, he had a prophecy and it didn't come true, so I began to doubt his prophecies. Then I doubted his ministry and finally doubted my healing. It was after that that the cancer returned.'

'It's clear that you were healed when he prayed for you,' I answered, 'and I think that you must start believing now that you were healed then. That you must do by faith.'

Looking at the wreck in front of me the question arose in my mind — how can he have faith? I voiced it without meaning to, 'How can you have faith?' and with that the answer rolled off my tongue, 'Faith cometh by hearing, and hearing by the word of God.' I didn't at that time know the niceties of the translation of *word*, the variations between the Greek *logos* and *rhema*, but the Holy Spirit, who was evidently in control, constrained me to put it this way.

'You must begin to read the word of God. Don't read any part of the word though, read those portions on healing. For instance . . .' Now, I found myself quoting two or three scriptures on the subject, but was interrupted by the sight of the man, a perplexed look on his face, slowly raising his left arm and then thumping himself with a single heavy stroke on the chest.

'The pain,' he explained in a low voice and almost breathlessly, 'the pain, it's going — it's actually going. Listen,' he continued with growing excitement, 'let me tell you about myself.' This he did for a couple of minutes, then turning to his companion, he said, 'The pain, it's gone — it's actually gone.' With that he lunged forward, threw his arms about me and embraced me warmly.

I found Elizabeth moments later and explained in perplexity what had happened.

'I know about the laying-on of hands,' I said, 'about anointing with oil and the prayer of faith. I didn't do any of that, though: I just quoted a couple of scriptures to him and he was apparently immediately healed.' In the distance we could see the man, standing bare-headed, hands raised to heaven and face radiant as he praised the God who had so remarkably touched him.

The next day I was doing the daily reading in my Bible. It was Psalm 107 and in verse 20 was the record, 'He sent his word, and healed them.'

The subject of physical healing became one of particular interest since the results were quantifiable in the clearly defined terms that appeal to a scientist. We were, though, to discover that the process did not necessarily follow a well-ordered and pre-determined route that the scientist might like, nor was healing going to be the result of a certain set of mechanics undertaken by those taking part. It was a consequence of the grace of God and we needed to hear what the Lord was saying in any particular situation. Without the word from the Lord we were in danger of trying to turn the Christian experience into a mechanistic action/reaction system, probably doing a lot of damage on the way.

While we were living in Derby, we were approached
by Philip, one of our closest friends, whose vibrancy for
the Lord was infectious and whose experience stretched
for well over a generation.

'We would like to bring Sheila to your home for prayer,' he said. Sheila was a talented young lady, much used
of the Lord in singing to her own guitar accompaniment.
She had, however, suffered from infantile paralysis and
walked thereafter with two leg-braces and sticks. It was
for her physical healing that a small group of us were to
gather around this, as usual, serene figure.

The appointed evening arrived and, feeling a little
self-conscious, about half-a-dozen met with Sheila. We
agreed how we would go about prayer using scriptural
principles throughout and we began the meeting with
much praise. Gently, we moved towards that moment of
laying-on of hands as the Bible teaches and, as it seemed
appropriate, we prayed for her as prescribed.

Then came the step of faith and Sheila stood up without her walking sticks. She walked slowly up and down
the room, supported from time to time by those who
walked with her. We continued to pray and praise the
Lord while there was not much sign of a physical improvement in Sheila who was unused to such exercise.
We next reasoned that the only thing to do was to encourage her to remove the leg-irons. This she did and
then eager hands drew her to her feet. Leaning heavily
upon one and another of us she made her way painfully
across the room, but was virtually carried most of the
way. We couldn't understand it: Sheila wasn't walking,
yet we had prayed and acted in accordance with what we
understood the Bible to say. We prayed yet more, weeping before the Lord and we walked Sheila for hours
until, tearfully, we had to admit defeat. Sheila walked
away from the house in her leg-irons probably feeling
very hurt, as we were.

For weeks I felt bruised, even let down by the Lord
and then, one day I heard a prophecy being given to
Sheila by a visitor to the area who knew nothing of our

efforts.

'You will walk physically,' said this stranger, 'as you learn to walk spiritually before the Lord.'

Slowly it dawned upon me that the Lord God is the final arbiter in this, as in all, matters. He had now given the word to indicate the way in which his grace would be demonstrated and all that we did would not force him into a corner to a different plan; how vital, it was becoming evident, for us to hear the word of the Lord in any situation and then to be obedient to him.

While my faith seemed, for the moment, somewhat damaged, I found that not only was I drawn into a more vital form of relationship with the Lord, but the ministry of physical healing, as a sign of God's love, was not rejected or discarded. Many questions still remain unanswered and the cynic will remain cynical, but over the years there has been a large body of evidence to demonstrate that the Lord has not abandoned this evidence of his love toward his people.

5

Prophecy and Its Performance

'Isn't it exciting that you've arrived in Derby just a week before the meetings at which Dick Carter will be speaking?' enthused Beryl.

'Oh, yes,' we replied, attempting to reflect the brightness of her moment and, following a short embarrassing pause added, '. . . but who is Dick Carter?'

'He's a man with a tremendous Holy Ghost ministry,' we were informed and, once more supporting our end of the conversation, looking full of anticipation, we said, 'Isn't that good. . . but what is a Holy Ghost ministry?'

With sweet sympathy on her face and just a touch of mystery in her voice, she responded, 'I think you'd better come and find out.'

A few days later we arrived for the first meeting. Few people were yet there, although it was to fill up, but the speaker for the evening was immediately evident. Dr Richard P. Carter was an American, as anyone who saw him would be convinced. He wore an electric blue suit, had crew-cut hair approximately a quarter of an inch long and weighed about twenty-five stone. He was standing alone, not far inside the entrance to the building and, as we entered, I thought that, though I was a visitor to this church, I should greet this visitor to the United Kingdom. Walking over to him, I extended my right hand and we exchanged pleasantries. In the moment my eyes caught his, though, there was the overwhelming sense that this man was not looking at me, but into me. I was transfixed by the steady, unblinking, yet loving gaze and became aware, as seldom ever, of the presence of the Lord God. For many seconds, perhaps ten, maybe twenty, I stood in silence looking at this unexpected intruder into my life, then coughing, I smiled and said that I'd better find a seat — there were only a few hundred empty ones available just then!

The service began, not following the sort of pattern to which we had become used over a lifetime, but highly truncated in content and very lively in expression. The pastor led a hymn, enthusiastically conducting his congregation, urging first this section and then that to sing louder. With arms waving encouragingly and his strong Welsh accent, he might have been conducting the assembled multitudes at a rugby international at Cardiff Arms Park football ground. He followed this with a short prayer and within minutes of the start of the service, Dick Carter was speaking.

Our exposure to Christian ministry had, thus far, been the Bible study and the regular Sunday morning service in our Fenland village. Never had I heard anything like that evening though: it was as if liquid gold was being poured out from the pulpit and with hungry fascination I devoured all for an hour and a quarter that seemed like ten minutes.

As he wound up his address, the speaker said, 'Those of you who must go, must go, but the remainder of us will stay for the after-meeting, where we will seek God.'

What an after-meeting was I didn't know, but I had just seen what a Holy Ghost ministry was, and that had been pretty terrific, so we decided to continue with this evening of discovery. In any case the idea of seeking God was both novel and interesting.

Only a couple of people left, while the remainder sat still in what seemed to be a heightening anticipation. Within the congregation, Elizabeth and I were fairly well to the back, sat on remarkably comfortable, red velvet pop-up, theatre seats. The speaker descended from the large pulpit area to stand on a smaller raised platform closer to his audience. Hands crossed in front of his ample frame, he stood quietly for several moments before pointing to someone in the front and on the side of the congregation in which we sat.

'Would that couple step out to the front?' he asked. Before us were a number of couples at any of whom he might have been pointing. Whoever it was, it seemed strange to me that he would choose to greet somebody at that moment, when he could have kept his socializing until later. Perhaps this was why this sort of church was called nonconformist: they certainly didn't appear to conform to any behavioural pattern I recognized from my church background. Or perhaps it was because he was an American and they just did things differently. No one moved.

'Would that couple please step out to the front?' he repeated. Now his pointing hand was raised rather higher and I realized that I had been mistaken: he was pointing to someone behind, not in front of us. The pop-up seats always signalled movement with their soft thud as the occupant stood, but there was no soft thud behind us. Slowly I looked over my shoulder . . . there was no one behind us!

'That young married couple,' the speaker was now quite insistent, 'will you step out to the front please?' I froze as I saw his finger pointing straight at Elizabeth and me. This time there was no movement since the strength seemed to have gone from my legs.

In consternation the speaker turned to the pastor of the church and said, 'They are married, aren't they?' The pastor looked confused, as he didn't know us.

'Do you mean us?' Eizabeth was standing addressing this strange American and as he, in relief, confirmed it, my wife seemed to drag me out of my seat to march me to the front.

I was acutely embarrassed to be standing before a large, expectant crowd of total strangers and lamely took his right hand extended towards us.

'You're finding all this rather strange,' I heard him say.

'Too right,' I thought. 'The world of science is my domain where unemotional calm prevails and I move from one situation to the next knowing where I'm going and what I'm doing. I don't mind, if that's the way it's to be, going to church on Sunday, reading my Bible, having a relationship with the Lord, even seeing the occasional miracle, so long as it's all done quietly and in order, but I think I draw the line at this sort of exposure, when I haven't the remotest idea of what is going to happen.'

'But,' he went on in his American deep-southern drawl, 'you've been asking the Lord a question.' Indeed, we had. For nearly three weeks we had been asking the Lord what we were to be doing in Derby. We had thought primarily in terms of the church we should attend. We'd been to the local church but realized immediately that theirs was not our gospel: I had recognized the characteristics of a Christ-less social message with no spiritual meat. Our pilgrimage had taken us all around the Derby ring-road to the next church where we sat under a Bible-based word at the end of which I heard, to my surprise, the Lord speak in my heart, saying that this was not to be our spiritual home.

We had continued to say in prayer, daily, 'Lord, what are we supposed to be doing here?' No one else knew of that prayer except the Lord.

My astonished ears heard this man repeat the content of that prayer, after which he said, 'And this is the Lord's answer to your prayer. Thus saith the Lord . . .' Once more my analytical mind was taking a battering as revelation poured forth, words of direction, of encouragement and of love. '. . . your ministry will be in your home,' I heard him as through a daze. 'Strangers will come to your home, people whose lives are on the rocks and whose marriages are on the rocks and they will come to you for help, there will be meetings in your home . . . and this is the beginning for . . .' he continued.

We returned to our seats, knowing that in a most remarkable way we had heard from God, but not yet knowing that within the space of one year we would see the execution of every element of that prophetic word.

Two evenings later I was working in the conservatory

of my home. One of the many car engines was the subject of my attention when I happened to glance up, and looked along the drive that led to the front gate. Two people were walking towards the house, a man and his wife whom we had not previously met, total strangers, except for the fact that I recognized the husband to be a Rolls-Royce employee whom I had briefly encountered in a corridor at the company offices one day.

'Goodness,' I thought, 'it's begun!' Indeed it had, for having been invited into the sitting room, coffee having been made, they were in moments telling us about the fracture in their marriage relationship. What, if anything, we did for them I shall never know, but I do know what they did for us: by being in our home, they not only confirmed the prophecy that we had heard less than forty-eight hours previously, but also underlined for us the principle that prophecy was relevant not just to a nation, three to four thousand years ago, but to those who would hear the Lord God today. That was to have an eventual effect upon our lives beyond anything that my logical mind could conceive.

★   ★   ★

The next few days were largely used in ruminating over the events leading up to and including the prophecy. Here was a dimension in the Christian life whose existence we had not even suspected. It hadn't been so long since Elizabeth had been saying, 'I knew that God spoke to people in Bible days, but do you mean that he speaks to people now?' Since then we had been precipitated through a series of revelations, each one destroying to some extent my fondly held rationalistic philosophy of life. God existed, the Bible was relevant, prayer worked, lives could be changed, bodies could be healed: now, though, we were faced with the fact that as God spoke to Abraham and Isaac, Moses and Joshua, Elijah and Elisha, and through them to nations and individuals, he could and might speak to us.

It was the following Thursday evening that the front-door bell rang. There were one or two Christian friends standing at the door to visit us, so the coffee pot was soon bubbling. Again the bell rang and there was another friend. After the third time the bell rang we noted with surprise that the sitting room was well filled with seven or eight Christians.

As people rose to go home, I suggested that we might have a prayer together and this we did, thinking no more of the evening than that we had never had so many Christian visitors at one time before. The next Thursday, however, it happened again, not with the same group of visitors, although some had been in our house on the previous week. This time we drank coffee, read a short passage of scripture and then prayed together before the evening was over. The pattern was repeated the following week, when the Bible reading took greater prominence. It was about that time that we recalled some of the words of that prophecy, 'meetings will begin in your home.' They had and they continued, without any invitation ever being issued, over the whole period that we lived in Derby and later they were to follow us as we moved south almost a hundred miles to Bedfordshire.

A year later Dick Carter returned to the United Kingdom and to Derby. Eagerly, we went to the church at which he was speaking and, with an anticipation we had not known on the earlier occasion, we listened to every word. As the meeting drew to a close he again called us to the front, but this time there was not the reticence on our part: the word of a year ago had been proved, point by point in detail and now we wanted to hear more from the Lord God in this way. Could this itinerant American possibly have remembered us and that earlier prophecy following a year in which he had moved around the world, speaking in a kaleidoscope of churches, fellowships, conventions and meetings? Certainly the word that he brought tied up exactly with what we had heard previously and now expanded upon it, pointing toward growth in our lives and experience.

Reference was made to the meetings in our home and, with that reference, a note of caution, 'Someone will come to your home and try to infiltrate the meeting with heresy. They will bring tapes to your home for you to listen to and this is a warning . . .' we heard. That was rather worrying, but also an intriguing variation on anything we had previously known. Always the word of prophecy had been overtly positive, had brought encouragement, manifesting the love of God in a clearly recognizable way, but this was different and certainly remained in our thoughts.

A couple of Thursdays later, the meeting was under way when the door bell rang. There stood on the door step a remarkably small man with a remarkably large, black Bible: it dominated him.

'I hear that Christians meet in this house,' he said.

'Yes,' I replied and pointing to his Bible, continued, 'and I see you have brought the right passport. Come right in.'

His name was Jack and he'd come almost eighty miles from his home. We were amazed that anyone eighty miles away had even heard of us and even more amazed that a person would make that trip to be at a Christian meeting. Certainly he had something to offer. As we continued to share our feelings about the scripture under review, he began to add constructive comments, share experiences and generally enthuse us. He returned the next week and the next, taking an increasing part in the proceedings.

After about four weeks of Jack's visits he arrived, not on a Thursday, but on a Monday.

'I won't be able to be with you on Thursday, ' he said, 'but I thought the group should listen to this tape.' So saying, he handed me a cassette tape. In my head, bells rang and red lights flashed as I heard an echo of the prophecy of six weeks before.

'Someone . . . will bring tapes to your home . . . this is a warning.'

'Thank you, Jack,' I said. I don't promise to play it, but I'll certainly listen carefully to it before doing anything else.'

Could this be that of which we had been warned? Indeed it was and as we listened to the recorded message we heard distorted interpretation of the scripture that would have led us clean away from the path along which the Lord was taking us. With thankful hearts we learned that God was able to keep us from falling.

The days of discovery, begun in Hemingford Grey, continued in Derby and particularly at the weekly meetings in our home. We now had no David to lead us and in some ways we seemed to be on our own. The best that we could manage to begin with was to follow a Bible commentary, but we found that as soon as we opened it everyone yawned and as it was closed, everyone brightened up. Raw beginners we might have been, but it was clear that God was going to have us wait on him for an understanding of what the Bible was all about and, in particular, what he wanted to minister to our hearts.

From time to time a non-Christian was brought by a friend and often the result was our rejoicing with the angels as the victim of the evening was converted. Bill was one for whom we prayed much. Elaine, his girlfriend, who had come to the Lord some weeks before, brought him. He was not to be moved by such Bible exposition as we could offer and certainly he seemed quite unimpressed by the witness around him. Week by week we prayed for him and our consternation grew upon hearing of Bill and Elaine's engagement with arrangements for marriage in the near future. Bill remained inscrutable and unmoved, except that he seemed to get progressively more morose in his demeanour.

We had just about given up, having exhausted whatever armoury we felt was at our disposal, when a Billy Graham Crusade came to England, centred upon London but with relays at major cities around the country. Nottingham, close by, was the site of a relay, and Elizabeth and I involved ourselves in the work of counsellors. Late one evening, the meeting over, we were walking back to our car through the soft evening light outside the stadium where the relays were held when, about twenty yards

away, Bill and Elaine walked around the corner. One
glance at Bill was enough: he glowed and the memory of
those silly grins on the film 'Souls in Conflict' came back.

'It's happened,' I whispered to Elizabeth, 'look at Bill!'
We all greeted one another warmly. A blow-by-blow account of the evening was given with rejoicing as they
relived the moment of the new birth. We later said
goodbye and didn't see them again.

After seven years had passed we had an air letter from
New Zealand:

'Dear Roy and Elizabeth,' it began, 'We don't expect
you will remember us . . .' We could never forget Bill
and Elaine and as their story unfolded in the letter, lives
that had been led by the Lord in Africa and then further
east and south to an eventual home in New Zealand, we
realized that when the Lord Jesus said we should have
fruit and the fruit would remain, he meant it. Years
later I was speaking at a church in Auckland, New Zealand
and there, in the congregation, was Elaine.

★   ★   ★

Mary had begun coming to the Thursday evenings some
time after they commenced and there were two important events in her life that typified the meetings.

David, our close guide and friend in Hemingford
Grey, was our guest in Derby for a few days. Thursday
had come and the meeting had passed when a small
group of six or seven of us stood in a circle to pray. We
were still very hesitant in our expression and David was,
as always, urging us on.

That hesitancy was displayed in a rather long silence
as we stood in prayer and the silence was broken by
David's rather stern command, 'Speak the word that the
Lord has given you, sister.'

Now David thought that Elizabeth had a word from
the Lord and so he, with us, was surprised when Mary
spoke, 'My God, my God, why hast thou forsaken me?'
words from Psalm 22 repeated by Jesus at Calvary. At
that Mary fell, as if pole-axed, right across the centre of

the circle, her head miraculously passing through an eight-inch gap between the lethal edges of a coffee table and a chair. No one moved — we didn't, in any case, know what to do — so we continued praying as if nothing untoward had happened, the body lying in front of us.

There seemed to be some reluctance to finish the prayer time since it meant that we would have to do something about the problem of Mary, inert on the ground. As we looked up in some embarrassment, Mary stirred herself, raised herself, and we all went home. We were not to know that the following Tuesday she was due to go to hospital for some delicate internal surgery. When she presented herself at the hospital, the pre-operational checks revealed to the surgeons that there was no good cause to undertake the planned operation: Mary had nothing wrong with her. It seems that the surgery had been accomplished on our living-room floor five days earlier.

Mary's marriage had been deteriorating for years. John, her husband, had no interest in her new-found Christianity: indeed it seemed as if his tendency towards manic depression was merely heightened. That, coupled with a very volatile temper, made him difficult to live with and, time and again, as his fibre snapped, there would be a great row terminating in his leaving home to go for a wild drive in his car that lasted some hours.

It had happened before and it happened again on the occasion of a Thursday night meeting, only, this time, instead of staying at home by herself, Mary had Christian company to whom she could go. She arrived rather tear-stained at the meeting and with wringing of her hands, she told the sad story of her marriage. There was nothing that we could do other than assure her of the Lord's love and pray for the situation.

'The problem is,' she told us, 'that when he goes off in his car in one of these rages, I've no idea if I shall ever see him alive again, he drives so recklessly.' At least we could intercede for that, and, having mustered our faith, we prayed that John would come to his senses, that he would not be involved in a car crash and that he would come to the Lord that evening. All of our reason assured us of the impossibility of such a set of happenings.

Just after ten o'clock, people began to spill out into the night but, having left, one returned to tell me with some concern that a car was parked in darkness outside the house and there appeared to be someone inside it. A glance through the bushes assured Mary that this was her husband's car and now she again became tearful at the thought of further quarrelling. I suggested that I go to meet her husband first and she should wait in the house for a while.

Walking to his car, I opened the passenger door, got in and greeted John cheerfully. As I closed the door behind me, it was as if the heavens opened with a rainstorm of unprecedented fierceness. There was no way in which anyone could either leave the car or approach it. It was necessary almost to shout to be heard above the noise of rain beating on the roof and my greeting didn't meet with a promising response. The conversation was, however, maintained and soon he was talking about his problem, and I of the Lord. Rapidly, the heart of this desperately unhappy man was melted, we bowed our heads and he asked the Lord into his life. No sooner had this happened than, just as rapidly as it had started, the torrential downpour of rain ceased, as if a tap had been turned off. The front door of the house opened, Mary hurried along the path, getting into the car as I got out and, with her new-born husband, drove off.

Years later I was approached by a heavily bearded man at the end of a church service. A stranger to me, yet with vaguely familiar eyes, he had the radiant look of a Christian who knew his Lord. Introducing himself, he asked if I recalled the evening in the car when he was born again, and once more the thunder of the rainstorm filled my ears, as warmth filled my heart in the knowledge that the fruit remained.

6

Conversions in Cambridge

Only a short time had passed since the dramatic period in Hemingford Grey when we had been challenged by God to give our lives to him. Now, though, I was becoming increasingly aware that the demands he made upon me and his interest in me could not neatly be contained within prescribed compartments as I had initially hoped and practised. The embracing nature of his interest had obvious advantages but also had far-reaching consequences that weren't so desirable to one who had successfully steered his own ship, made his own decisions and was, by his own thinking, quite capable of continuing that way. The importance of the Christian life and message may have broken in on me in the days following my conversion but the rational mind was at work all the while determined, even unconsciously, to subvert the authority that the Lord might claim. As I had assessed my position, I soon determined that Sunday, the prayer meeting, those few minutes every morning and maybe certain special events were his, but my career, scientific interests, vintage car activities (which by now had become fairly intense), family affairs, holidays and general decisions in life, were mine. But this division of my life could not continue, and the erosion of my kingdom became at times painful, for no man wants to lose what he has won. Relinquishment was made all the more difficult because I was not fighting a foe who I could hit back at and whose superior forces I would yield to only as the world looking on might acknowledge the injustice: this was a Friend who evidently loved me, yet demanded a price — everything.

We were now living in Derby but the contacts with Hemingford Grey and the surrounding district were being maintained. We knew of an evangelistic campaign in that area and decide to support it by being present over one weekend. The Saturday evening service was not particularly well attended so I had no difficulty in picking out my friend Kenneth, the bank-employee who had been converted in our home. With him was a man in his mid-twenties under whose arm was a Bible of impressive dimensions.

After greeting Kenneth, I was introduced to the bearer of the Bible, Tony, and, in the slightly charged atmosphere of a crusade, had no difficulty in asking him brightly, 'When did you become a Christian?'

'I have not become a Christian,' he replied sourly, 'I am an atheist who is here as a guest.'

The Bible under his arm, he assured me, was not his, but had been thrust upon him as he came to the meeting. The wind having been taken from my sails, I proceeded more cautiously as he told me of his background. His parents were atheists whose free thinking had not been free enough to countenance the existence of God. Their principles had been impregnated in Tony who had never even entered a church building once in his life.

By now we were standing in the open air beneath a cloudless dark sky punctuated by innumerable stars.

Swinging his right arm expansively above him, he declared with an air of finality, 'I can't believe that a thinking mind was behind all that.'

Tony may have been in control of the discussion — he was certainly in control of his philosophy and appeared to be in control of the world with its associated galaxy — but he had one problem: he had no means of travelling the ten miles back to Cambridge to his college. Kenneth volunteered that I would drive us all back into town, although I was staying for the night in the opposite direction. It was grudgingly that I agreed: a warm bed was more inviting than a late-night tour of the Cambridgeshire countryside. Telephoning my wife, who was now enjoying supper with members of the mission team, I explained the situation, but there was something else that worried me and called for discussion.

The following weekend I had no intention of being at the mission for it was the date of the annual rally of the vintage car club of which I was a committee member and magazine editor. This event, to which I looked forward every year, was not to be missed, but I certainly didn't want the Christians at the campaign to know why we wouldn't be joining them. In consequence, Elizabeth had been carefully trained to use a form of words in which any invitation to be at the meetings over the following weekend would be declined 'because of a previous commitment.' Over the telephone this was, yet again, carefully rehearsed with Elizabeth before taking Tony and Kenneth into Cambridge.

As we drove along the Roman road connecting Huntingdon and Cambridge, an enthusiastic Kenneth announced that it was time to pray. I'd never prayed at 60 m.p.h. before, and, being the driver, wasn't quite sure what to do. Clasping my hands wasn't going to help the car's steering and closing my eyes seemed positively dangerous. We survived Kenneth's prayer however, and I acknowledged it with a lame, yet thankful, 'Amen'.

Kenneth's enthusiasm continued to rise and when, upon reaching Trinity College, Tony invited us into his rooms for coffee, Kenneth's keenness knew no bounds.

The car parked, we climbed the echoing staircase to Tony's rooms, Kenneth by now singing at the top of his voice, 'Expect a miracle every day; Expect a miracle when you pray . . .'

Doors opened and astonished faces followed our progress as I quietly longed for the earth to open and swallow me up!

Finally, we were seated in a small, but pleasant student sitting-room, small enough to make Kenneth's loud singing quite unnecessary. Tony opened the discussion making several assertions, yet probing, questioning, anxious to reconcile his firmly held and logically presented views with the claims of the two idiots before him. His was a sharp intellect, able to quantify arguments, assess the corollaries, deal with the objections and amass further arguments to justify his position. He was one of the youngest research fellows in Cambridge and for a good reason. In despair I knew that this was not a person who would easily be brought to faith of any sort, for the concepts of faith were too simplistic for him, yet I also recognized that to argue along his philosophical lines could not bring anyone towards the Lord. Kenneth's chorus sung on the stairs was a mockery: I couldn't expect a miracle in this situation, yet, how little did I account for the working of the Holy Spirit for, to my surprise, a miracle we saw.

For an hour and a half the conversation continued, the dialogue degenerating into a monologue as Tony's questions became seemingly unanswerable. They were answered, though, but in an unexpected way.

A question asked, there was a pause, then Tony would say, 'But I suppose your answer would be . . .'

With relief we agreed, this then being met by a further conundrum which, after thought, Tony again answered.

So he continued, driving himself remorsely into a corner until finally he said, 'I am convinced. I want to become a Christian. Now, what do I do?'

Startled by the turn of events we tried to advise him. Without further ado, he knelt upon the carpet of his sitting room, bowed his head, gave his life to the Lord . . . and was born again.

There was to be a sequel of which we couldn't have been aware. Some weeks later I was back on one of my frequent trips to Cambridge from Derby to do some work in one of the many libraries of the university. Having difficulty in locating a reference, I obtained the help of one of the library assistants, a young woman whose needs were so obvious that, moved with compassion, I began to talk to her about the Lord. To demonstrate a point, I took my New Testament out of my pocket to show her a verse. I later learned that, seeing this, the lady nearly took fright and ran, considering me to be deranged. The few moments over, I picked up the reference I needed and left the library.

The seed had been sown however, and over the next few weeks there was awakened in Ann an intense desire to meet the Lord of whom this stranger had been talking. It was several weeks later that I was again in Cambridge and, walking into the same library, was surprised at Ann's warm welcome. She was anxious to help, following me along the corridors created by regimented, tall bookcases. Soon we were talking about the Lord and in moments I recognized a prepared heart, so asked her if she would care to pray. Eagerly she agreed, but where? The stockroom was the only place and longing that the nodding heads in the library would keep nodding, but feeling a million eyes boring into my back, I followed Ann into the privacy of the stockroom. We prayed and as she looked up, I knew that there was no doubt about it: she had met Jesus!

What could I do with her though? The church in Hemingford Grey was ten miles away and she had no transport. The number of my Christian days in Cambridge before moving to Derby could almost have been measured in single figures so no contacts had been made. Overtures from the Cambridge Inter-Collegiate Christian Union had long ago been firmly resisted by me when I had first gone up to university. I knew not one Christian in the whole of Cambridge, except Tony, and I hadn't seen him in a while.

'Here's a name,' I said scribbling on a piece of notepaper. He's in Trinity and this is his room number. He's a Christian: at least you have can have fellowship with him.' At that I had to leave.

My visits to Cambridge became less frequent and it wasn't until a month or so later that I was in that library again. Ann was there and I enquired of her progress. Yes, she had been growing in Christian things, but slowly. She was looking for a church to make her home and she had visited Tony. No, she didn't see him again, nor did it seem likely. There was not much more I could do, beyond pray.

It was almost six months later that we met again. Ann was now integrated into a lively church, she was involved in Bible study and prayer and, to my relief, all was well. But what of Tony? I hadn't had contact with him in a long time, so very tentatively I enquired if she had ever chanced to meet him again.

'Oh yes,' Ann volunteered, 'As a matter of fact I'm meeting him for luncheon today.'

In response to my evident surprise and joy she added, 'I'm sure that you'd like to know, we're being married in three months time!'

★   ★   ★

Kenneth and I drove out of Cambridge elated. Tony was the first person that I, as a Christian, had seen give his life to the Lord and I began to understand something of the joy of Christian service. I had been called to forfeit my evening, my supper and a substantial part of my night, but the relinquishment had had its reward. Kenneth's chorus-singing became a duet in the car and a choir in heaven, so it was in high spirits we parted and I made my way to David's home where Elizabeth and I were staying overnight.

I crept into the house expecting sensible people to be abed, but heard quiet talking in the sitting room. Slipping through the doorway I found Elizabeth and David in prayer. David was in the middle of a prophecy which, in a gathering of two seemed a little unusual but was, in his ignorance, a total of three following my silent entry. The words were profound, but I was arrested by an inclusion in mid-sentence, and apparently out of context:

'. . . go and be baptized . . .' There was little doubt that David hadn't heard me creep into the room, but there was no doubt that the word was for me. Rebellion flared up in me: I may have been born again, but that had been into a denomination that didn't subscribe to that sort of thing. It had been enough to go through one intellectual humiliation in becoming a Christian so there could be no justification in a further resignation of intellect in getting wet all over and pretending that this was, in some way, edifying. Besides the only baptismal service of which I knew was scheduled for the following weekend when I was determined to go vintage car rallying.

The glory of the evening turned to misery as I knew, once more, the convicting hand of God upon me and the misery continued as I fought what I would have liked to think was a theological battle over baptism, but was in fact a last-ditch defence of the sanctity of my weekend with old cars. The old cars lost the argument and I knew that my right to myself was slipping away.

So it was, that, five or six days later, we returned to Hemingford Grey and I was baptized, not in a beautiful baptistry surrounded by a reverential audience, but in a portable swimmimg pool made of flexible corrugated tin, whose owner kept complaining about people damaging the sides, while the congregation let rip with the sung statement, 'It's no longer I that liveth, but Christ that liveth in me.' Even if what was being sung was, to me at any rate, largely theoretical, there had been a little dying that night.

★   ★   ★

It had been a long evening, for quite a few baptisms had taken place and then, after the service, there had been lengthy fellowship. Mary had been there to rejoice with those who had been baptized but was anxious to return home where her unconverted husband waited. My offer to drive her the couple of miles was accepted and when we reached her house her husband was out. We prayed together for a few moments before I returned to the car to drive off. I pressed the starter button but the engine would not fire. Minutes passed as, time and again, the starter motor whirred without response. With annoyance I remembered that the flashlamp had been left at home and I couldn't possibly attend to the engine in the darkness of the night. As time progressed, I had the vision of an irate unconverted husband returning home from the

pub to find an unwelcome man, who had escorted his
wife home, outside his house. In my mind, the scene
developed until he took a swing at me and he flattened
my nose. Returning to my senses, I knew that something
had to be done and quickly, but I was also aware that in
the darkness there was nothing I could do. In my memory was an incident recounted earlier that weekend when
a co-worker, Slim, so named because he wasn't, had apparently addressed a locked door commanding it to open
in Jesus' name . . . and it had. That story had been beyond all credibility: doors and locks were inanimate ob-
jects, so they couldn't even hear what was being said,
much less respond to the instruction. The whole thing
was totally preposterous, yet Slim had been both sincere
and jubilant in relating his story. Could it be then that
the name of Jesus had dominion over things as well as
people?

There was nothing else to be done and it was with a
sense of being drawn into something from which I would
rather have been a long way away that, clearing my
throat, I addressed the dashboard of the car (if the thing
had a brain I thought it ought to be about there), and
not knowing what form of the name of the Lord would
be acceptable in this particular circumstance, I used
every one I knew, 'In the name of Jesus Christ of Naza-
reth, I command you to start'.

Singing choruses on the staircases at Trinity had been
the height of reason compared with this, but feeling
charged with a tentative sort of faith that was mixed with
the embarrassment at hearing my own voice, my finger
pushed the starter button. The car started immediately.

I drove through the country lane, elation and wonder
filling my heart by turns. My engineering senses were
reeling: what could have gone wrong with the car I had
built with my own hands and yet had been set right only
by prayer? Approaching a major road I slowed, going
progressively down through the gears when, on the
over-run, there was a cough through the carburretor,
characteristic, in that car, of one thing: there was no fuel.
The engine continued to run, though, as I unearthed

the spare can of petrol from the boot and poured it into the empty tank. Something strange was happening that I could observe, quantify and that could only bring me to one conclusion. I, an engineering scientist, whose speciality was in engines and who knew intimately their operational characteristics and why they worked, had driven a car with no fuel in it.

★　　★　　★

We drove back to Derby through Rutland on country roads that became very familiar as we traversed them almost every week. Strange things continued to happen with the car. On one occasion, in heavy rain, the wind-screen-wiper motor, always a source of trouble, stopped. Elizabeth and I prayed as we drove: it started. Relieved, we stopped praying and it then stopped working. Alarmed, we prayed again, and it re-started, and so it continued all the way to Derby from Hemingford Grey: as we kept praying it kept working.

The big-end bearings on old cars, those vital and highly stressed components that transmit the power to the crank-shaft while permitting it to turn, are made of a low-melting point material and need a lot of oil to avoid melting in their hostile environment. The noise resulting from a molten big-end always gives a hollow feeling in the stomach of the enthusiastic owner and that certainly was the feeling I had, as, on yet another occasion, we were making our way back to Derby in the night hours, when the characteristic knocking added itself to the engine note. Elizabeth and I prayed in desperation and kept driving, albeit with a little less pressure on the accelerator. The noise disappeared.

It was with the greatest relief that we reached home and as soon as there was daylight I was stripping the engine. The oil was drained, the sump came off and gingerly I ran my fingers over the connecting rods. The offending rod being found, the locking washers were eased back, the bolts loosened and the cap taken off. Before my astonished eyes, there was presented a sight I had never seen in years of vintage motoring. The white-metal had gone from the cap almost completely but had left a ridge of unmelted bearing surface, traversing the critical region and no more than a sixteenth of an inch wide. The load which was normally supported on a bearing surface an inch and a half wide had been carried by one only four per cent of that required! I was coming to a clearer understanding that the God to whom I had turned just a few months before was intruding into my life at every point and confounding my reason in a beneficial, yet disturbing manner.

7

The First Pulpit And The Flying Witch

The meagre lifestyle of those student days, living on a grant, made impossible such indulgences as holidays for an increasing family. Other research students disappeared in July only to re-appear months later talking of far-away places. To me, though, Bournemouth was as strange a sounding name as Bangkok, but I consoled myself that my research was important and rewards would come with the development of the career.

So the appointment with Rolls-Royce heralded a new era and a family holiday was again possible as the bank account began to look more healthy. Elizabeth and I discussed with some anticipation what we might do and we resolved to return to the location of our previous holiday seven years before, Challacombe, a tiny village in Exmoor. Things were different for us then. On the earlier occasion there had been the two of us, Elizabeth carrying a healthy bulge that was to become Matthew: now we had two children, and were Christians just five months old.

We arrived at our destination, a small hotel nestling in a fold in the moorland and, after dinner, having put the children to bed, we enquired of the location of the parish church building. It was outside the village and finding it, we read the notice-board to discover that morning service was held there on the first, third and fifth Sundays of which the next day was one.

So it was that we arrived twenty minutes before the service was to commence only to find the place deserted and the door locked. A ten-minute wait convinced us that a mistake had been made somewhere, but, as we were leaving, cars began to arrive, a key was produced and we all filed in.

Elizabeth's keenness took her to the front and the rest of the family followed while the few others who had arrived disposed themselves around the building in an attempt to look like a crowd. A man began to hand-crank the organ bellows, a lady played an introit and it seemed as if we were about to enter the well-oiled pattern of service that had fitted that building over the centuries just as favourite old shoes fit the feet. Yet that was not to be so. I had prayed a little, looked round, noticed the vestry door to the left of the sanctuary and thought idly, 'In about three minutes the vicar will appear, probably at great speed with cassock and surplice flowing about him to emphasize the importance of the moment and his own busy life.'

A voice clearly responded, inside me, 'No, he won't. He's not coming today. You're preaching the sermon.'

The effect was petrifying! It was three minutes before the commencement of the service, but if that was the Lord speaking, he had certainly got it wrong. I had never preached and the thought had not entered my head that I ever would: I knew nothing about homiletics and precious little about the Bible. The idea was therefore quickly dismissed from my agitated mind as an aberration.

The minutes ticked by and then a lady from the congregation walked over to the organist to have a quick conversation before leaving the building.

After a short while she was back, there was another quick conversation with the organist and then she walked across to us to say, 'I'm sorry that we're late in starting but the vicar has to drive over from another church on the moor. I've just phoned his vicarage and there was no answer, so he will be on his way.'

Elizabeth smiled her thanks and I went white. It was now five minutes past the hour and I knew, as surely as I knew anything, that he would not be in Challacombe that morning. My mind raced in all directions as I tried to work out what one does in preaching a sermon. In the confusion I recalled that people usually seemed to start by quoting a verse of scripture then building upon it. That seemed to be a good ploy but with horror I realized that I could not think of even one verse of scripture: the Book which had been challenging me for five months might as well never have been opened! Nervously, I asked Elizabeth if she could recall a scripture about bread and stones and scorpions and, as she reminded me of Luke 11:9–13, she watched quizzically as I thumbed in a half-frenzy through my Bible looking for the elusive physician. He was lurking in the New Testament.

In a further minute or so, the lady who had made the phone call had yet another conversation with the organist who spoke to the pumper. He stopped, she closed the organ lid and the one who was clearly in control walked over to us apologetically.

'I'm so sorry,' she said, 'the vicar hasn't arrived, so we can't have a service. It really is embarrassing, for this has never happened before and it would occur on the day we have visitors. You see, we don't get visitors here.' Elizabeth and she continued in conversation as the congregation dutifully walked out and we moved towards the door.

'Don't say a word,' I instructed myself silently and forcibly, 'and no one will ever know that you were disobedient to the Lord.'

I had not accounted for the Lord knowing and acting, though. As we traversed the aisle I felt the hand of God coming upon me as never before: the conviction of disobedience was awful, almost as a great weight, but my rational mind continued to fight.

'There's no way now in which anyone will come back into the building for a service and, apart from that I don't know how to broach the subject,' I reasoned. But there was a way and they would return.

Standing on the pathway in the sunshine, I observed, 'Isn't it a pity when you think that we've all come to church to worship the Lord, but because one man doesn't turn up, we all go home without that worship?'

'Yes, when you put it that way, it does seem a pity,' she replied.

'I know,' I said, summoning up all the valour I had, 'why don't we sing a few hymns together, and say some prayers, and if you like I'll preach the sermon?'

Our new-found friend looked a little surprised but quite interested: Elizabeth looked at me as if I'd landed from Mars and was bleeping with flashing lights. 'That's a nice idea.' The stranger's enthusiasm was becoming visible, 'Let me have a talk to the others.'

So saying, she caught them at the lych-gate and they engaged in quite intent conversation. I stood in silence, trying to look entirely unconcerned, making sure that I could be seen by their eyes darting in my direction but keeping far enough away that I couldn't hear the conversation.

She returned, smiling, to say that everyone liked the idea but the churchwarden's permission would be necessary: he was by then little more than a dot on the horizon.

'George,' went up the strident cry and the distant figure turned to return. A short conversation with the lady and then he was shaking my hand to thank me for the offer of my service.

We returned to the building, but I had no idea what was going to happen. My mind was full of Luke 11:9–13 (I dared not forget it now), but my reverie was shattered as I was handed a hymnbook and asked to select the hymns. It dawned on me that I wasn't only about to preach my first, and almost certainly my last, sermon: I was also about to lead the whole service, sermon included! My knowledge of hymnbooks was even more scanty than that of the Bible, but I recalled an important principle of management: delegate.

'You choose the hymns,' I encouraged the organist, 'you know better than I what this congregation can sing.' Authoritatively, I added, 'We will have three hymns.'

We did and between the first two hymns there was a time of prayer. Then the moment came to preach. Luke 11:9–13 put in an appearance and knowing no more about the Bible, I told the story of what had happened in Hemingford Grey. The congregation seemed very interested.

About halfway through, a voice within said, 'The vicar's going to come through the door any moment. Aren't you going to look a fool when he does?' This, I recognized was not the voice of the God I served, so rejected it and survived the time uninterrupted.

We were about to flee at the end of the service when George insisted that I accompanied him to the vestry.

'Sign here,' he said, so to this day, in the space marked 'Celebrant', Challacombe Parish Church Register records my precipitation into a world of preaching.

Precipitation it was, for a week later in Derby there was a telephone call, 'Gordon here,' said a much-respected Christian member of the local County Hall, 'I hear that God has called you to a preaching ministry. Now, I organize two Methodist Circuit Plans and I'm going to put you on them.'

A few weeks later I began circuit-riding by speaking at a Sunday service in Staffordshire. I knew that I wasn't in the habitat of philosophers: my friends at Cambridge might have been on another planet (indeed I hoped that they were), but that first evening one-third of the congregation gave their hearts to the Lord to be born again and that made it all worthwhile.

★   ★   ★

'I don't think that we should go on this camping holiday, Roy.' It was a little over a year later as Elizabeth spoke to me with some concern. The plans had been quite carefully laid and were part of a strategy to cover two years. I had wanted to go to Poland to meet George, the Professor of Concrete and Reinforced Concrete with whom I had first shared a room in Cambridge and who now lived in Warsaw. The only way we could countenance such an adventure was to drive across Europe, camping by night. We had never been under canvas though and weren't quite sure how we would manage it, so had decided to experiment by camping in Wales, moving from one beautiful location to the next. I had the vision of glorious sun-lit mornings, sausages sizzling and coffee brewing on the stove as we read our Bibles and shared our quiet times together, the soft warm evenings beneath the canopy of God's creation and of course, on Sunday, the chapel in the valley. To this end a tent had been hired, our only guide being the glossy brochure and a floor-plan with an area marked 'Bedroom' in which were outlined three bodies neatly laid out. The children were small enough to go end to end and thus, we figured, this was the tent for us. Now, the day before we were to set out, Elizabeth was having second thoughts.

'I do feel that I've had a word from the Lord.' She went on,

'As I was praying I saw a hand which just closed and the Lord took me to a verse in my Amplified Bible which says, "God seals up . . . the hand of every man . . . that all men whom He has made may know His doings [His sovereign power, and their subjection to it]."'

'Nonsense,' I retorted, using rational argument and anxious that the plans should not be disturbed, 'if the Lord didn't want us to go, he would have told us before I had hired the tent and paid the deposit. We shall go.'

We went. The holiday began in a black mood as we found that all the equipment needed for camping didn't seem to fit into the car. We owned a three-litre Lagonda whose impressive eighteen-foot length terminated in a boot which became crowded when carrying a box of matches. Clearly, this car had been designed for those days of elegance when the trunks were sent ahead, planted along the route to mark staging posts for the grand-touring family. That certainly was not the Peacocks' scenario, but finally the pots, pans and first-aid box were stored in every known space around the vehicle by 4.00 p.m.

I was determined at least to get to Wales that evening and would have considered anything else a failure, so it was just about dusk when we found a camp-ground just over the border. Our dues paid, we were directed to a field of about ten acres on a steep slope and occupied by one tent. From its position I realized the pattern that would be made by the orderly ranks of tents filling the field as the evening wore on so set our tent tightly close to the other, the guy ropes just about crossing. Just one other tent arrived that night to fill the ten-acre field!

When darkness fell, the family of the next tent, including a child with a bad cough, returned. Our first discovery of camping is that canvas walls don't keep out sound and the child's cough kept us awake until about midnight. There then arrived the third tent and its occupants; a coach load of sea-scouts who were very hearty and noisy. They were finally quietened by their leader whose voice would have put a ship's horn to shame.

Shortly before 5.00 a.m. the dawn chorus of sea-scouts woke us. I had spent most of the night hanging on to my bed on the steep slope and now I was to discover that boiling a kettle and frying sausages were next to impossible on such an incline. Wearily, we began packing and six hours later, nerves frayed, we were ready to go. We determined to avoid organized camp sites in the future and the next night was spent in a field high above Pwllheli. It rained heavily: I had abandoned sleeping in the euphemistically described bedroom for lack of space and was in the outer tent under a window whose flap was broken. All night it rained on me. The next night was spent outside Caernarvon in a delightful spot surrounded by glorious ferns. As the sun set, the mosquitoes rose and with our own blood we generously fed the local squadrons that zoomed in on us. We then went inland to camp on Cader Idris, an impressive mountain. That night the winds were so high that the tent began to disintegrate around us and I had to move the car to create a windbreak, lashing the tent to the door-handles. If this was the Christian triumphalism of all the testimonies I had heard, then victorious Christian living was not for me.

Finally we were in Aberdovey, a small seaside town, trying, almost in exhaustion, at 4.00 p.m. to arrange some luncheon. We sat on the beach leaning against the sea-wall at the foot of the promenade fifteen feet above us, where the car was parked.

'There they are,' a voice seemed to come from heaven. 'Hello there, Roy, Elizabeth!'

We looked up and in astonishment saw Hilary and Chris, two ladies from the church we attended a hundred or so miles away. 'We've been looking for you everywhere,' they said, 'the Lord has given us a word for you and we knew that you were somewhere in North Wales. Then we saw the Lagonda parked here and knew that no one else had a car like that.'

Walking down the steps to the beach, they added, 'We feel that the Lord wants you to give up camping. Go and find a hotel, then enjoy yourselves. What's more we're going to pray that you'll find one immediately. Feeling suitably chastened, I obeyed and in minutes, at the first enquiry, we found an excellent place for the remainder of our holiday. The sun came out and we lazed on the beach watching, day by day, storm clouds a few miles away while we acquired enviable sun-tans.

The lazing gave me time to think. Elizabeth had had a word from God which my rationalistic mind had rejected because he apparently didn't work within my domain of reason. In straight disobedience (I hadn't even asked the Lord myself), I had insisted that we should go on the arranged holiday. It had been an unmitigated disaster until two ladies had come over a hundred miles with the word which we obeyed. What was more I knew that the probability of meeting those two ladies by chance in that way was statistically so remote that this had to be the hand of God. No longer were even my holiday arrangements my own: he wanted control. I determined to listen to his voice in future and I was equally determined never to be under canvas again.

For the next nine years there was never a summer vacation when we weren't engaged upon Christian work — camping in tents!

Christian camps in the United Kingdom just have to be a latter-day cross between medieval torture and primitive concepts of penance. My main memory is not of spiritual enlightenment, but tents so close that the guy ropes overlapped, facilities, particularly lavatories, hopelessly overloaded and an attitude among camp leaders, suitably ensconced elsewhere, that was insensitive and demanding. An exception was the series of Youth Camps at Lee Abbey, a Christian community in North Devon just a few miles from the venue of my first preaching engagement. We became part of the team over three years.

Our introduction to the Lee Abbey camps was a little unusual. Ray lived in the same village as us, after our move from Derby, and with his wife were regular attenders at the midweek meetings in our home. One evening he mentioned in prayer, a camp of which he was commandant. As he did so there was, unexpectedly, a strong witness of the Holy Spirit in me that we would be on the team for the coming year. Elizabeth also had that witness and so, separately did Ray and Pam, his wife. None of us mentioned it to any other, everyone believing themselves to be the only recipient of the Lord's word and waiting to learn that, in due course, the others would get the revelation. Besides, we all knew that the team places were fully spoken for. Elizabeth and I finally confided in each other and felt so convinced of the Lord's will that we didn't arrange anything else for that first summer. It was just three weeks before the camp began that a tentative comment passed between Pam, Ray's wife and Elizabeth and suddenly we were all agreed. Almost immediately another family had, for personal reasons, to cancel arrangements to be on the camp and the newly vacant places awaited us.

Arriving at the camp for the first time at 2.00 a.m., we had the sort of introduction I didn't want. As I pulled back the cover of our prepared bed, I found the largest black beetle in the world sleeping where I should have been sleeping!

We worked on three camps, each one, we learned, containing a fair number of young people who were active in the occult. I knew there was something wrong in such interests and was, by then, aware of the warnings

given in the book of Deuteronomy. As we kept to scriptural principles over those camps though, we saw many
delivered, as confession was made to involvement with
ouija boards, glass-pushing, astrology and witchcraft.

One year it seemed as if everyone had what they called
blockages. One man was challenged over ouija boards:
while he didn't use them he mentioned that he sold them
and, in consequence of prayer, he was immediately released. On the same day another grown man, upon enquiry, admitted a lively interest in horoscopes and then
was immediately delivered, again through prayer.

The most extraordinary events, though, concerned
Greta and Yvette. Upon our arrival at one camp we were
told that Greta was active in witchcraft while her friend
was an acolyte of hers. These two became a special subject of prayer for us.

A feature of the camps was the evening epilogue, the
only mandatory event. Different people spoke night by
night and so the content was variable, sometimes funny,
sometimes spiritually challenging. Every evening, from
the back of the assembly, I watched Greta: in times of
fun, she was fully involved in the proceedings, but as the
focus came upon Jesus she would appear, seated in her
chair, to slip into a form of trance. In due course it was
my turn to speak, when I had been invited to put out a
gospel challenge.

The focus of the selected theme was that Jesus was
declared to be the Son of God with power by the Holy
Spirit. Greta was seated on my extreme left in a 180
degree arc of campers and from time to time I glanced
in her direction. The response was as had been seen
before as, progressively, she slid lower in her chair, her
head hanging further back until, of her face, only her
chin could be seen. As we approached the climax of the
story, from the corner of my eye I caught the sight of an
unexpected movement. Glancing to my left, my astonished eyes saw Greta flying horizontally through the air,
probably three to four feet off the ground. It was as if
this attention broke something, for she immediately collapsed in a heap on the ground with a noisy thud. What-

ever the reason, it was annoying to have the continuity of the address broken at that moment so, as everyone looked at the source of the noise, I called their attention back, telling them to forget the girl lying on the floor.

After a further five minutes or so, squeaks began to emit from Greta, growing in intensity, until they could no longer be ignored, so I stopped speaking. Here now was a situation of which I'd read in the Bible yet seeming to have its roots in the uninformed understanding of medieval man. Although Greta certainly was strange in her behaviour, witches belonged to another age, flew on broomsticks and owned black cats with glowing eyes and strange powers. In an enlightened twentieth century, and I was one whose life had been spent in search of and extension of that enlightenment, phenomena attributed to witches were discounted and psychiatrists had quantified the aberrations that a previous age had misinterpreted. Yet before me over the last week there had been a person whose reaction to the name of Jesus had been curious and consistent. Evidently she was unable to control this, which clearly had a profound and immediate effect upon her life. Moments before, I had seen her defying gravitational laws and flying, not even ballistically, but in a horizontal path indicating that she hadn't jumped but was under the influence of a constant force. Now she was emitting inhuman noises rather like those of a very loud mouse. Where the Lord was taking me, I didn't know: this was not a well-established path of reason, but something had to be done. Calling the campers to pray, I saw the form on the ground begin to squirm like a snake as I walked to her. Voices began speaking out of her, one high-pitched, another a low growl, a third of yet a different character.

'Don't let him pray for us,' said one.

'Get us out of her quick,' said another.

Quite suddenly I was filled with an indignation and faith for the moment and at three separate commands, three demons left the girl, each one throwing her into the air to some extent. Greta was carried, apparently unconscious, into the chapel tent, where attempts were

made to take several amulets and charms off her. Even
with her eyes closed, she seemed to be able to watch and
counter every action throwing, at will, six grown men
around the tent as they tried to hold her. There was just
one more demon we understand, but by the next day,
Greta was in her right mind.

It would have been nice to think that the whole incident was just a bad dream, such was the assault on my
scientific mind: it could then be rejected and I could
concentrate upon those aspects of Christian theology
that brought intellectual satisfaction rather than be drawn
along this very non-rational path. There are two reasons
why this couldn't be the case. One is that the whole
evening was recorded on tape and there, undeniably,
are the voices of the demons set in a ferrous oxide film
as a continual reminder of the reality of Satanic power.
But the second reason is the important one: 120 people
witnessed the incident and that night forty of them came
to the Lord in repentance and were born again — a
more lasting record than that of magnetic tape.

★   ★   ★

Yvette was now alone. Her involvement, as far as we
could see, had been entirely with Greta and events had
taken an unexpected turn. She became the subject of
concentrated prayer and on the last evening of the camp
was still entirely miserable in her wretchedness. Following the last epilogue, one of the team members, Mike,
sat to talk with her. His loving nature produced a good
foundation for counselling and knowing that time was
to be spent with her, he had asked me to wait around in
case of developments.

It was at 2.00 a.m. as I was pacing around to keep
awake that Yvette asked for prayer. Mike signalled and I
joined them. Several questions were put to Yvette to
confirm her position and all were answered quite satis-
factorily. It was then that my eye was drawn to a curious,
yet not flamboyant, necklace with a small carved elephant
on it around her neck.

'What is that?' I asked innocently, aware of the disturbing nudge of the Holy Spirit within me.

'Just a necklace,' she replied.

'Nothing more,' I enquired further, 'It's not an amulet, is it?'

Her answer in the negative gave no comfort and then my eyes were opened to the fact that she had lied and all her answers were also lies.

'You have a lying spirit,' I heard myself say, 'and the only prayer that I will pray will be for your deliverance.'

After a further talk when the battle clearly raged within her, Yvette agreed to this prayer. She bowed her head and was immediately delivered.

Looking up, she took the necklace off and, handing it to me she said, 'It is an amulet. Will you get rid of it for me, please?'

We then went back over all the earlier questions and the answers were substantially different, but the atmosphere was now one of truth.

Giving the amulet back to her, I said, 'Yvette, you shall have the pleasure of getting rid of this thing yourself. Let's go down to the field-kitchen.'

Below us was a small, open-sided building which housed both the open fire upon which all the cooking was done and the three boilers, glorying under the names of Matthew, Mark and Luke, that provided the hot water for washing, sterilizing and even making tea. The fires were kept in night and day and the smoke exhausted through three chimneys about fifteen feet high, poking through the corrugated iron roof. We walked into the kitchen area, located the hottest boiler-fire, opened the fire-door and Yvette threw the object in. Because the chimneys were at such a height, there were never any fumes from those fires in the kitchen itself, but, on this occasion, as we stood back, we were all quite overwhelmed, just for a moment, with a most disgusting smell before the air cleared. Yvette was free and I had some thinking to do to quantify the unambiguous events of that fortnight in particular and of our recent holidays in general.

8

House-Hunting

The move to Cambridge, four years before our conversion, had been surrounded with difficulties. There had been the almost impossible problem of balancing the finances we had, with the costs of an affordable home that was adequate for meeting the needs of a family which included a baby a few weeks old. Then there was the incompatible demand of University regulations stating that I should live within three miles of, of all places, the porch of Great St Mary's church at the heart of the city. Fortunately, it was in ignorance of the existence of that rule and even of the existence of Great St Mary's church that we moved into Hemingford Grey: the battle with the University had followed shortly afterwards.

In moving later, as brand-new Christians, to Derby, we had begun to gain a faint inkling of the interest that the Lord had in every aspect of our lives. It was for us a curious thing to do, but we did pray about the move, asking God to lead us to the house we were to have. Having lived in an East Anglian village we had a pretty good idea of what we felt we could aspire to and laid out our shopping list carefully: a Georgian house set in a village-type of environment. Our hopes were dashed upon visiting the first estate agent and learning that in the Derby area, such properties did not exist. It was, however, shortly afterwards that we learned, through an old friend, of a house for sale close to his home. We saw it and bought it. It was all so natural that it didn't seem as if it could have been an answer to prayer and it was only when we came to sell the house some years later that we realized, by its strategic location, this had certainly been the Lord's response to our prayers. Having been precipitated into a life in which we had discovered much that was overtly supernatural, it would have been easy to have discounted such events, natural in their situation and development, from being answers to prayer.

We had lived in Derby for two or three years when we saw the Lord opening for me a significant career development in joining the faculty of a technological institute that was a post-graduate university. This meant a move south of about a hundred miles, leading to the sale of our house in Derby and the acquisition of another somewhere in Bedfordshire.

Simultaneously, one house went on to the market as I began the search for the other. At first things looked as if they would move quickly: a couple came to view the Derby house and said that they would let us know what they wanted to do.

As they walked down the drive, Elizabeth confided in me, 'They're going to buy this house.'

'How on earth do you know?' I asked.

'The Lord just told me,' she responded sweetly. This was marvellous, it must be what the Christian life was all about, I thought: no more worrying about such things as property transactions for, as soon as we began to move in the Lord's will, it would all happen in a smooth, well-oiled manner. A week later it was, therefore, a major disappointment to hear that the couple weren't going to continue with the purchase. Over the following weeks there was a steady stream of enquiries and pseudo-purchasers, yet only one further person showed any interest and he became a major problem. He had, over a period of time, no fewer than six surveys done on the house, after each of which he negotiated a lower price, but never moved towards purchase.

He was finally despatched because, in the words of the agent, 'If we ever get him to a table to sign a contract, he'll find that he has no ink in his pen.'

There may have been some irritating moments as

potential purchasers, one after another, toured the property, but that was not nearly as unnerving as the period that followed when nobody came. Had we made a huge mistake? Was this the work of Satan? Questions of this sort filled my day, but as I prayed, I had no doubt that the Lord God had pointed me to my job, so at least in arranging to move the family we couldn't be wrong. Complaining to the Lord, I asked him why the house was not selling.

Speaking within my heart, I heard him say, 'It doesn't sell because you don't trust me to sell it.'

'Of course, I trust you Lord, that's why I'm praying,' was my indignant response.

'If you trust me to sell the house, why then do you have it in the hands of an agent?' came his word.

'Because that's the way it's always done,' I responded.

'Take it out of the agent's hands and I will sell it for you,' the chilling words formed within me.

'Oh Lord, I cannot do that,' I explained, 'Elizabeth could never take such an action. It's bad enough, our being apart almost all the time, but if I take the house from the agent's hands it will make the sale seem impossible and the likelihood of us being together even more remote.'

After further contemplation, certain that this would be an end of the matter, I added, 'I could only do this, Lord, if you told Elizabeth yourself, and I could only recognize that as your word if you spoke it to her before I get home on Friday.' Then completing my point, I said, 'And further, if this is your will, let it be the first thing that she mentions to me when I get home.'

Friday afternoon came and I drove back to Derby where, on the doorstep of the house, I was greeted by Elizabeth.

'Has the Lord said anything to you this week?' was her first comment.

'Maybe,' I said, 'has he said anything to you?'

'Roy,' she was looking serious, 'you'd better come in and sit down. Now, please don't get angry with me, for I don't think that you're going to like what I have to say.'

We sat and she continued, 'I think the Lord has said that we must take the house out of the agent's hands and he will sell it.'

I didn't know whether to laugh at getting such a clear confirmation from God or cry because of the enormity of the step to which I was called.

The house came off the market and we waited. Nothing happened. I went to the Lord and, again complaining, I asked why the house was not sold.

'It doesn't sell because you don't trust me,' I heard the voice.

'But, Lord, I do. I asked you to sell it, then when you told me to, I took the house off the market. Of course I trust you.'

'If you trusted me, you'd take down the agent's "For Sale" notice.'

'I didn't think that you'd notice that, Lord, but it's his sign and his job to take it down.'

'Take down the notice and I'll sell the house.'

Grudgingly the sign came down the following weekend and I laid it in the garden where, just possibly, it might be seen. We waited and again nothing happened. Once more I was before the Lord in the matter, when one day Elizabeth telephoned me, 'Roy,' she said, 'I think that I have a word from the Lord. It's in Ezekiel 12 and I think that you'd better read it.'

With one house for sale I had to find another in which we could live. This had always been a tedious pastime to me and even though I was seeking the Lord this time it made the occupation no more pleasant. Slowly I worked my way through an enormous pile of brochures and most evenings would drive to some point in Bedfordshire where I would view a couple of properties. In praying, I became convinced that the Lord wanted us to live somewhere in an arc of nine or ten villages that stretched from Woburn to Ampthill and so I confined my hunting to these places.

One evening, I had been to two houses in the village of Aspley Guise but, even as I rang the door bell at each place, was certain that the Lord was saying, 'It's not here.' In both instances I dutifully followed the owner around before politely bowing my way out.

As I returned to the hall of residence in which I stayed at the Institute I ran over things in my mind.

'Now I've no doubt that God has brought me here,' I said to myself, 'and I know that it is a principle that he intends families not to be separated. Therefore he intends that we should be united and that must mean that my family should be with me. Since that can only happen if we have a house of our own, I must conclude that he has a house for us somewhere. Why isn't he showing me the house?'

In astonishment I heard his word come to my heart, 'He's not showing it to you, because you're not giving him a chance to. Stop rushing around looking for the house and he will bring it to you.' I could hardly believe such a command but by the time I entered the dining-hall for a rather late dinner my mind was made up.

'How's the house-hunting going, Roy?' asked Alan, a new-found Christian colleague.

'Well, it's rather interesting: the Lord has told me to stop house-hunting and has said that he will bring the house to me,' I replied. Alan looked at me with evident concern.

'Roy,' he said, 'You know that I respect the stand you make for the Lord, but you must be sensible about this. Go out and get a house — get it anywhere — then move your family down here as soon as possible and get on with the Lord's work.'

'Alan, you're expressing my sentiments entirely, for that's what I feel like doing. But I have to be obedient to what I believe the Lord has said to me,' I replied.

So house-hunting stopped and, on Friday I went home to tell Elizabeth the news. She didn't look at all happy about it. The next week I waited and nothing happened. On Friday evening I was greeted by a wife whose face looked a little longer. It continued that way for a total of three weeks by which time we knew that our faith was being taxed to its limit.

On the fourth Monday morning, as on others, we rose early to have an hour of prayer, before I drove off for the week. As I prayed I said, 'Lord, you know that we have been obedient to your word and have waited now for three weeks. Honour our faith this week by showing us the house, please.'

Certainly, at that stage of our Christian lives we felt that three weeks, which seemed close to an eternity, was long enough to wait for anything.

The week proceeded as before, until, early on the Wednesday evening, I was in my room preparing to go to dinner in the refectory below. It occurred that the Lord would have to show me the house by next evening, because on the Friday I was to return to Derby. I didn't doubt that that would be so but I thought, 'He's leaving it a little late.'

At that moment there was a knock on the door and the porter announced that I was wanted on the telephone. At the telephone I heard the voice of a Christian man I didn't know, though I had met him for a few minutes some weeks before.

We talked about nothing for a while and I was wondering the purpose of his call when he said, 'I feel that I should tell you about a house I have for sale.' So saying he related the details and my hair stood on end. We had asked for nothing like this: there were so many rooms and so much ground that it sounded more like a castle than a house.

He terminated his description, 'Do you think that you are interested?'

I was not: nothing could drag me to a property like that, but as, in a second or so, I reviewed the conversation, one thing stood out — the timing was perfect.

'Well, yes,' I replied cautiously and at this, Eric, the man on the telephone, suggested that I might look at the house. I knew that if this was of God then it should be the next evening that I would see it, so was then rather confused to learn that he had an engagement at that

time. A date was fixed for the following Wednesday and
rather complicated details were worked out for our
meeting.

As everything was finalized, the vendor surprised me
further by saying, 'I don't suppose you could make it
tomorrow evening instead of next Wednesday?'

My mind was in a whirl as I agreed the new date, rang
off, then telephoned Elizabeth. 'Don't get excited,' I said,
'but it's just possible that the Lord is showing us the
house that we are to have. You pray and I'll have a look
at it.'

The next evening I walked around the house with
Eric and his wife who lived close by. The large property
which I explored was empty and seemed positively cav-
ernous with no furniture in it. There was no opportunity
to give a report to Elizabeth when I got home on the
Friday: she pre-empted any discussion, greeting me at
the door and waving an envelope on the back of which
she had scribbled half-a-dozen scriptural references.

'The Lord has shown me that this house is for us,'
she exclaimed joyfully, 'look at these verses I have.'

'Don't bother to show them to me,' I replied rather
sternly, 'if God wants us to have this house, he's going to
have to speak to me directly.' So it was, for on the following Monday evening as I prayed, the Lord gave me verse
after verse. Many months later, Elizabeth and I were to
discover that the same verses had been given to each of
us.

I visited the house-owner during the following week
and told him we would buy the house.

'But,' he said looking rather surprised, 'we haven't
discussed the price yet and, in any case, your wife will
want to see it before such a decision.'

'The price is the Lord's responsibility,' I replied, hop-
ing that the Lord would note that, 'and it's not necessary
for Elizabeth to see the house, for we feel we've heard
from God. Nevertheless, she would like to see it.' A day
was set for later in the week and, as we drove to his
home we prayed that, as a confirmation and to show that
this was not a product of our own hearts, the Lord would

speak directly to him.

We arrived at his house and were ushered to a table and chairs set in a small attractive garden. On the table was an open Bible.

We sat and Eric opened the conversation, 'I've asked the Lord for a word,' he said, 'and this is what he has given me. It's Esther 4:14: "For if thou altogether holdest thy peace at this time, then shall there enlargement and deliverance arise to the Jews from another place; but thou and thy father's house shall be destroyed: and who knoweth whether thou art come to the kingdom for such a time as this?"'

He looked up and into the middle distance over my shoulder as he repeated, ' . . . and who knoweth whether thou art come to the kingdom for such a time as this?'

Focusing his eyes upon me he said, 'There is something that I should tell you about this house — it's jointly owned by me and my father-in-law. I think that you are to buy it.'

I turned to Ezekiel 12 and read the Lord's injunction as he had given it to Elizabeth in Derby and she had repeated it to me by telephone: 'Remove . . . thy stuff; remove . . . in their sight; remove . . . in the evening.'

The word was clear: step by step the Lord had led us in progressive relinquishment. We had taken the Derby house from the agent's hands, the notice-board had come down and now he was calling us to leave the place. But houses devoid of furniture don't sell easily and this was at a time when vandalism was growing rapidly. The prospect was daunting, yet we had been drawn into a position from which there seemed to be no withdrawal. If we ignored this injunction, declaring that it was not of God, how were we to determine that anything we had received may have been of him? If all those other words were not of him, but had been the fabrication of over-active minds, we really were in a mess: it almost seemed easier to take the next step forward than to take all those backward,

retracing the path we had travelled. Yet to leave the
house empty, knowing the danger of vandalism, the reduced market appeal with no furniture present — and
being fully aware that this pile of bricks and mortar represented all that we owned of a tangible nature in the
world — was frightening. With heavy hearts we made
the arrangements to move and found that the only time
that was convenient to the furniture removers for picking up our belongings was in the evening. It was wryly
interesting to see that even that detail of the scripture we
had read in Ezekiel 12 was being fulfilled.

In preparation for living in the large, mainly seven-
teenth- and eighteenth-century house to which we were
moving, arrangements had been made to have all the
timber in the structure treated against wood infestation.
We didn't know the problems that that would create, but
we began to find them as we arrived at the house half-
way through the next day. We were met in the street by
the son of the vendor, who, looking very agitated, gave
us the bad news that the electricity board's electricians
had been there earlier to switch on the power but had
found that every circuit in the house was leaking to earth
because the old fabric-covered wiring had soaked up
most of the wood-preserving fluid. As a result, they re-
fused to switch on the power. Entering the kitchen, we
met a man from the gas board. His job was to switch on
the gas for the heating supply, but since the boiler was
electrically ignited he was not allowed, for safety reasons,
to turn on the gas. We were reeling under this blow
when we heard footsteps on the stairs. It was the plumber
coming to tell us that he couldn't turn on the water because he had already found five burst pipes in just one
bathroom. No electricity, no gas, no water — we wan-
dered around the house stunned and walked into the
designated sitting room to find that it had no floor! Two
workmen looked up in embarrassment to tell us that
they had just found extensive wet-rot in the floor joists,
had tried to telephone me the day before, had failed to
contact me, but were replacing the whole of the floor
with new wood. We turned to what was to be the library

only to discover that it was awash with preserving fluid and there seemed nowhere left to put our furniture that was less than an hour behind us on the road. Eventually we were forced to use a large upstairs room for which we had never seen a purpose but, when furnished, became the family drawing room: for other reasons, it would become known to some as the Upper Room.

Night fell, blanketing the chaos of our removal in darkness. Beds had been hastily erected in various rooms but without any light we felt our way around to crawl between the sheets. It was in the depths of the night that we were awakened by the screams of our daughter. In the darkness we had several problems: we couldn't find the room she was in and we couldn't even find the door to get out of our own room. After several unsuccessful attempts at walking through walls we reached the landing, falling up and down odd stairs designed into the building as traps for the unwary, to find Rachel very sick in bed. She was carried back to our room and I spent the remains of a most uncomfortable night with the feet of a small child occasionally kicking my back in her sleep.

Over the next few weeks we had much opportunity to question if we had made a huge mistake. Everything possible seemed to have gone wrong. To get power into the house we had run a heavy cable through the ground floor to the kitchen and, in the depths of winter, this meant that we couldn't close the doors. We were utterly miserable, yet time and again as we checked on our actions we couldn't see where a mistake had been made. Further, Elizabeth now told me, that months before I had ever known about the house, she had been glancing through a newspaper and had seen an advertisement for an unusual house. As she read it, she had felt the Lord tell her that this was the house for us. So convinced was she, that she had visited Beryl, a Christian friend, to tell her the news. She was later to discover that the advertisement had been for the house to which we had come. In addition we had the comfort that we knew of friends who were praying for us and one of whom was given a vision of part of the house, which he later identified. But

it was Beryl who brought a special assurance at that time.
She had been in prayer a month before we moved when
the Lord had given to her a vision of a house in darkness
and in it, she knew there was a sick child. As she sought
the Lord, he said to her, 'Pray for Roy and Elizabeth,'
and this she had done, telling us of this remarkably accurate vision several weeks after the event.

★   ★   ★

We settled in and a semblance of sanity returned to our
way of life. Soon we had water, then electricity and then
gas and our lives began to take shape in these new surroundings. We discovered that there was, after all, a
purpose in being there. The house in Derby stayed
empty and daily it was the subject of prayer. We asked
the Lord to defend it and to sell it, though how it could
sell, we didn't know.

We had, one Saturday, spent the day away visiting
friends and upon returning home were surprised to find a
note pinned to the door. It announced that Pauline, a
friend of long standing from our Derby days had come
to see us and was waiting at a friend's house locally. I
went to meet her and she was evidently excited by some
news that she wouldn't share until we were home with
Elizabeth.

'You remember Jane, your close neighbour in Derby,'
she told Elizabeth, 'I've been baby-sitting for her occasionally. Last night she was going out with her husband at seven o'clock and I arrived at quarter-to-seven
to see the children to bed before the parents went out.
During the fifteen-minute period when both Jane and I
were there, the telephone rang and she answered it. I
heard her say, "I don't really know, but my baby-sitter
may be able to answer your question," and with that she
called me to the phone. There was a man enquiring if
your house was still for sale, saying that he was anxious
to contact you because he wished to buy it. I said that as
far as I knew it was still for sale, so took his number and
name, telling him that I would pass it on to you. I went

back to college that evening thinking that I might come to Bedford by train, but I noticed that the college hockey team had an away match in Bedford the next day and there was just one spare seat on the coach. I jumped on the coach, had a free ride down and here I am.'

We were excited by the news, realizing that if the phone call had been made before Pauline had got to her assignment at a quarter-to-seven that evening, the contact would not have been made and if after seven o'clock when the babies' parents were out, the question would not have been asked, for the enquirer would not have realized Pauline's relationship with us.

Contact with the enquirers was made and arrangements progressed for the sale of the house. When we met them, our astonishment knew no bounds — they were the first couple who had visited us a year before, whom the Lord had pointed out to Elizabeth as the ones who would buy the house. When they had been interested a year before, they had liked it but had been unable to sell their own home, so had dropped their interest. Now, though, the husband had been offered a new senior appointment with the Electricity Generating Board with whom he worked. This involved a new contract, one of whose clauses was that he must live within the city boundary of Derby.

'But our house is about a hundred yards outside of the city boundary,' I told him a little crest-fallen, 'that's why we always had low rates to pay.'

'It was when you lived there,' he told us, 'and when we looked at it first. It just happens that in the last few weeks there has been an Act of Parliament, steered through by George Brown, the Member of Parliament for Belper, Derby constituency and assistant leader of the Labour Party, which extends the Derby boundaries. Your house is now just inside the boundary.'

We had had numerous difficulties in that move from Derby to Bedford, but through them all there had shone, as it were, a beacon to assure us that we were in the Lord's will. At the darker moments, when there was personal discomfort and we seemed to be walking a precarious plank, there had been nothing more than his word to guide us, yet as we looked in retrospect we realized that he was backing his word with a succession of miraculous workings to achieve his will, getting us into the place he would have us be. It had been hard enough for me to come to terms with the fact that God seemed directly interested in so many areas of my life: when I realized that he was prepared to speak through circumstances and through friends, even that he would use an Act of Parliament at exactly the right time to achieve his purpose, I was awe-struck with the God whom it was my privilege to be serving.

9

Creation and a Cracked Head

'When we examine these early chapters of the book of
Genesis we have to understand that they were writings
in fairy-tale form, in an attempt to explain to primitive
people something about the nature of God. Today in an
advanced society we know that the Genesis story is not
true, science has shown otherwise, but when we see what
the writer was trying to do, there is still something that
can be gained from this. Now if we can have some discussion, please?' David, our pastor, was leading the midweek Bible study and we were looking at the scriptures
selected for the readings on the following Sunday. The
discussion moved slowly around the room, each person
making a contribution: schoolteacher, government official, housewife — a normal distribution of jobs and
vocations represented in an English village, but in the
whole room, there was only one person who would be
identified by academic background, industrial history
and career as a scientist.

That was me. I knew that a lot depended upon what I
would say about the Genesis story for, as a scientist con-
tributing to that body of knowledge that seemed intent
upon destroying the Bible, my life appeared to many as
a contradiction in terms — a scientist who seemed to
believe the Bible — or at least parts of it. My contribution
was going to shake some people I knew, but how could I
put it over in a way that would carry conviction rather
than a sense of pedantry. As I reflected upon this I
heard David's voice, 'Roy what do you think about this

reading?' I cleared my throat and decided that the only thing to be done was to tell of my voyage of discovery from its start.

At my conversion I hadn't believed any of the Bible. In my pre-Christian days before entering the atheistic phase of my life, I had read it, but it hadn't meant a thing to me. In fact, my Bible reading, which had lasted for some years, had been undertaken for strange reasons. In the church I attended we were expected, year by year to do something really sacrificial during Lent. In succeeding years I had tried most things that I considered sacrificial, which I had interpreted as 'unpleasant'. One year I had decided to give up sugar in all my beverages and although to begin with everything tasted dreadful I found, that, by the end of Lent, I positively enjoyed my tea, coffee and cocoa without sugar and have done ever since. Nevertheless while it may have done me good physically I concluded that I had gained nothing spiritually since I enjoyed it and the exercises of that Lent were written off as a failure.

The next year I felt that I really should do something that would be quite awful as a sort of penance and the most awful thing that I could think to do was to read my Bible. I therefore resolved to read one chapter a day. It was awful, so I concluded that it did me good and, as Lent finished, with the Bible reading seeming just as awful, decided that there was no reason why I should not continue to benefit: so I maintained the practice of reading one chapter a day.

The resolve carried me through a whole year until the next Lent when I was faced with the problem of doing something even more distasteful than the previous year. The only thing that I could think would be more awful than reading a chapter of the Bible every day was to read two chapters a day, so that became my style for the next year. Of course, scientists always extrapolate and I sometimes wondered with abject horror where this would all end, but fortunately I found my pseudo-atheism to be a convenient escape from the prospect of reading increasingly large portions of the scripture year by year.

Over the whole of that period, though, I do not recall any scripture having any impact upon me and cannot remember one verse that I read.

Upon my conversion, the Bible had come to life. The gospels were vibrant, the epistles were rich and the Psalms became the outpourings of the hearts of men like myself. Yet there was a problem. We had been brought, by the experiences we had had, to acknowledge the validity of claims laid down in the Bible of God's interest in a person's soul, of his participation in individual lives, of his intervention in the process of sickness to bring health and his involvement at other levels of life and relationship. Yet there were things that the Bible said which offended my scientific sensibilities and none was more dominant than the thought that God's activity was cosmic to the point of defining the nature of the universe. The whole body of science, which I could not ignore, led me to conclude that the earth was of immense age, and life, as we knew it, had developed over those aeons of time, being formed, mutated and reshaped by the environmental forces around it.

But this led me to a problem. Since there was no doubt in my mind that I had met and was privileged to have a continuing relationship with him, I wanted people to know about Jesus Christ. Yet the only reliable reference book that I knew, to which I could direct anyone in their search, was the Bible, whose opening chapters I didn't believe. In recommending people to read it I would find myself advising them to begin with one of the gospels, and at the same time deflecting their interest in a covert sort of way from the opening chapters of Genesis. In my secular work as a faculty member of an academic body I had several of my own students whose progress I encouraged and monitored closely. In addition there was a larger body of students who came to me for advice in areas of my specialization. Often, their enquiries could best be met in reading one of an innumerable collection of reference books which I might pull from a shelf to recommend. What sort of recommendation would it be though for me to say to my students, 'Read this: it will

answer your questions and clear matters up for you. Oh,
incidentally don't bother to read the first few chapters:
they're not reliable. In fact they are a misleading fairy-
tale.' I can only imagine that the student's confidence in
the volume given to him would have been shaken, if not
destroyed. If he couldn't believe the foundational chapters how could he believe the development? There is
every likelihood that he would turn elsewhere for the
resolution of his enquiry.

Then again, I had further difficulty. The scientist in
me was trained to define limits — the dimensional limits
between which a component of an engine may be considered satisfactory, the operational limits of an aircraft
or the limits beyond which a hypothesis was not arguable.
What now must be the limits of credibility in my Bible?
Certainly they could be set by defining the limits of incredibility. Now I knew that I had no problem over the
truthfulness of the gospels and there seemed to be no
problem over the fallacy of the Genesis story. Somewhere
between them there has to be a point at which I could
draw my line of credibility. But where was it? If I determined that Genesis 1 should be deleted from my acceptable canon of scripture, then certainly Genesis 2 should
go as well. The third chapter of Genesis carried the same
air of incredibility because it spoke of the original man
and woman described earlier and the fourth chapter
must likewise go. Disturbingly, with this progression I
was discovering two things. The Bible seemed to have
convincing continuity, chapter to chapter and book to
book — Genesis led smoothly into Exodus and Exodus
into Leviticus — so that I couldn't define my line at all
well. I was also discovering that my Bible was becoming
noticeably thin.

There was another approach that I could try and that
was to abandon the whole of the Old Testament: I felt
that I was on safe ground in the New Testament only.
But that, too, had drawbacks for the New was constantly
referring back to the Old, so if the Old was unreliable
could I claim reliability in the New?

Over a lengthy time I returned periodically to grapple

with this problem but never reached a satisfactory conclusion. One day, however, the question became even
more urgent, for I was faced with the most fundamental
threat to my belief and my relationship with Christ. I
had been reading the discourse in Matthew between
Jesus and some Jewish disciples where an argument had
grown over divorce. Moses' bill of divorcement had become the central issue, when, to explain himself, Jesus
said, 'Have ye not read, that he which made them at the
beginning made them male and female . . .?'

The words broke in on me and I knew that the challenge to me was not concerned with an ethic in marriage
or divorce but in the unequivocal statement that Jesus
had chosen to make, 'He which made them at the beginning.' My first thought, having acknowledged that his
was a masterly development of his thesis, going back to
roots in the best tradition of debate and philosophical
thought, was that Jesus believed there was a definable
beginning and an identifiable man and woman at the
beginning. My second thought was that, when he made
that statement, he was two thousand years nearer the
event than I was, so had more authority than I to judge
whether or not it was correctly reported. My third
thought was yet more basic. The Jesus who I had come
to know, love and worship had, thus far, shown himself
to be entirely reliable. I had not discovered in him one
lie or even shadow of turning. In this then I was faced
with the major challenge of my Christian life and I knew
that all that followed would be based upon my reaction
to it. If my assessment of origins was correct, a development of the universe over millions of years, whose physics obeyed the laws of science in general and thermodynamics in particular then it was a corollary that man
had ascended from some primeval accident, progressing
from form to form in response to the slow but irresist-
ible changes in the cosmos to his present position, then I
must conclude that Jesus was wrong. In fact, in his
unique position as the Son of the omniscient God, he
wasn't just wrong through misinformed nature — he
was a liar. On the other hand, if he was right then all

that I held dear to my heart about creation had to be wrong. Such were the incompatibilities that there could no longer be co-existence between my apparently scientific position and that of Christ, and a decision was demanded over which of these I would discard.

The battle raged in my mind. My commitment to the Lord had been such that this couldn't be abandoned out of hand, but my commitment to the widely propagated ideas of creation had been life-long. To lose the former was to walk away from the amazing spiritual discoveries of the last few years: to reject the latter was to be humiliated in acknowledging that I had been wrong over a lifetime and that might even affect the foundations of my science.

Finally, the decision was made. I admitted to myself that Christ knew more than I did so his was the voice of authority and I would thus commit myself to his word: I had been wrong in my life-long reasoning. Beyond making this commitment to his claim, I didn't know or understand how it was worked out. It was, however, a relief not to have to wrestle any more, but from that moment something strange happened. As I began to look afresh at my hitherto fondly held beliefs I began to discover that such foundational features as Lyell's Theory of Uniformitarianism didn't sit well alongside the Second Law of Thermodynamics. With excitement, I recognized that the Laws of Thermodynamics, basic to and immutable in the universe as we know it, supported, not a Lyellian model or a neo-Darwinian development, but the concept that I saw laid down in the book of Genesis! I pressed forward to make this into a proof, but found I couldn't, because the Second Law operated within boundary conditions — limits that I could not define. Nevertheless, I arrived at one important conclusion: I could accept the widely held views of creation if I wished — but only by faith, since the proofs offered were not convincing or I could accept the Genesis story by faith. As I embarked upon the latter, I found that beliefs, previously held to be without question, were being eroded.

The Carbon 14 method of dating was, I discovered, based upon a calibration curve that was extrapolated way beyond any limit that I, as an engineer, would ever contemplate. My confidence in dating techniques was shaken even further upon learning that Carbon 14 dating of Stonehenge had been re-assessed because of a 'hiccup' the calibration curve was discovered to have. While archaeologists were congratulating themselves that this increased the age of Stonehenge by about six to eight hundred years, thus matching the Phoenician marks on the stones, no one paused to acknowledge that the previously held assumption had been wrong by about 25% and that in comparatively recent history. Further, the evidence laid in fossils led me to believe that a 'Uniformitarian' model, such as is generally accepted, could not be valid. Most important, I could not now reconcile all that I had earlier learned with the Second Law of Thermodynamics. I was being led to the conviction that history consisted of one or more non-Uniformitarian events — the flood and before that, the creation. It was a day or so after my commitment to the clear statement of the Lord Jesus that I found the writer to the Hebrews to have declared, 'Through faith we understand that the worlds were framed by the word of God' (Hebrews 11:3). I was soon also to discover a further authority that the Lord Jesus had had in his statement to the Jewish disciples — according to John, he had been there in the beginning (John 1:1-4).

★   ★   ★

My story finished, I looked at the audience around the room. One or two were smiling, some looked concerned, but David, the pastor looked at me in open astonishment, 'You mean . . . you believe this?' he questioned falteringly and pointing at his Bible.

'I do,' I responded, feeling now quite firm in my ground and knowing a peace.

'You believe . . . all of it?' he probed, holding his Bible in front of him.

'All of it,' I replied.

'Does that mean we can believe it, too?' he enquired.

'I believe so,' I responded.

A look of realization and joy broke slowly across his face and then turning to different quarters of the room by turns, and holding out his Bible, he repeated slowly, 'We can believe it . . . we can believe it!'

★   ★   ★

'I wonder if you would like to join me in the ministry of the church weekend in two months time?' David and I were drinking coffee after the morning service, talking about his announcement that the dates for the annual retreat had been arranged.

As I responded warmly David went on, 'I think that the time will be spent in much deep counselling at a personal level.'

I felt a check inside at those words and after weighing them for a moment responded, 'If that is what you want, that's fine, but I think that I'll leave the ministry to you, David.'

Glancing enquiringly at me, he walked off to talk to someone else, but he returned after a few minutes to ask why I had so reacted.

'I don't really know, David, but when you used the words "deep counselling" I felt disturbed in my spirit and although I don't know what those words mean, I feel that it's wrong.'

'What do you think that we should do?' was David's next question at which I made the suggestion that we should spend the time around the word of God and let him direct us from there.

The idea took root, but I little realized that that weekend would play a part in the further working of God in my life through a series of incidents that were quantifiable in scientific terms.

We were all to gather at a location in Northamptonshire on the Friday evening. That morning I had gone into my office as usual at 9.00 a.m. knowing that I was to give a lecture at 11.10 a.m. My secretary told me that several of my students were waiting to see me — men working for their doctorate and Master's degrees who needed guidance and encouragement. One by one, they came into the office for discussion until, looking at my watch, I realized that it was just before 11.00 a.m. Ushering the last man out of my room and knowing that in minutes I was to be at a lecture-room podium, I ran to the washroom. Wheeling quickly around the door, I didn't notice that the tiled floor had just been swabbed and was wet. My feet flew from beneath me and I fell backwards. As a reflex, my arms went behind me but the back of my head struck sharply against a door post, throwing me forward. Head first, I was thrown against the sharp edge of a concrete window-sill, and as my forehead struck it I saw a dazzling, blood-red light that faded into blackness as I slipped to the floor.

Dick was a colleague who happened to walk into the washroom sometime afterwards where he heard a groan. Looking around he saw a pair of feet sticking through a doorway and, reckoning that was not normal, he investigated. He found me, head jammed between the wall and a lavatory.

My first awareness of life after the red light was to feel my feet being pulled and to hear an anxious voice say, 'I've got to get him out of there.' My jammed head didn't help matters but finally Dick extracted me and got me into his office to sit down. His concern was evident, but I suddenly remembered that I should be giving a lecture so, feeling rather fragile, staggered off.

After the lecture I felt very ill, so went home and to bed before having to drive to Northampton. During the evening I felt worse so was glad to get to bed for a rest before I began to minister the following morning.

The next day I felt dreadful as I woke and found that only my left eye would open. Going to the mirror I saw with surprise that the skin above my right eye had formed a bag, filled with blood, which hung down, covering the eye completely. I washed and dressed, the world swimming about me. It was clear that there was something very wrong and the whole of my metabolism was reacting.

In excruciating pain I entered the first session of the morning, taking a seat close to the door as I anticipated having to leave. David got through a few announcements and then introduced me as the speaker. Feeling quite nauseous I rose, but as I did so, something amazing happened: my head cleared, the pain left me, the nausea lifted and though I could only view the audience with one eye, I felt fine. Having shared the word, I sat down with some satisfaction but as I did so, to my dismay, the head pains and nausea returned in all their fullness. They stayed with me until I rose to speak at the next session when once again they departed, only to return as I sat down. So this continued over the whole of the weekend.

During the next three weeks, the head pain was my constant companion, changing as the days progressed from violent sharpness to a continuing dull ache. It was then as I was talking to the head of department, that he commented by way of an aside, 'I hear that you had a fall recently.'

Laughingly, I brushed his comment aside with the remark, 'Can you imagine it . . . I fell over in the gents' loo and knocked my head.'

'Did you go to a doctor?' he enquired.

'Of course not,' I responded, 'I don't need to be treated as an old man.'

His face took on a stern look and almost with a note of anger, he retorted, 'Don't you realize how dangerous it is to knock your head? You go to the Institute doctor at once.'

I had much respect, even a loyal affection for this man, and was alarmed at the firmness of the first order he had ever given me, so I walked over to the Institute surgery.

I entered the waiting room to find it packed with the wives of students all looking pink and pregnant and immediately felt rather out of place. The nurse at reception enquired why I was there, then looking quite alarmed, put me first in the queue. In moments the doc-

tor was asking me questions, feeling my head. He seemed
very concerned and instructed me to see my family doctor at once. I drove home and went to his surgery. In
moments the same evident concern was on his face and
in his words as he said, 'You are to go for X-rays at once
in Luton.'

A day later I was sat in the radiologist's waiting room
wondering what the problem really was. Did I have a
fractured skull and if so, what were the long-term effects? Would I have to live with this pain which was now
at a bearable, if unpleasant level?

The radiologist called me in and said that two views of
the skull were needed. I described where the impact had
been, the decisions were made and the shots were taken.
I was asked to wait for ten minutes or so while the nega-
tives were developed and checked. After a while the
radiologist emerged looking very worried.

'Will you come back for two more shots?' I was asked.
This time the head positions were different but again I
was asked to wait. Twice more the action was repeated
until a total of eight shots had been taken, all of different views. The radiologist would say nothing but didn't
look too happy and by now I was really worried.

The following day Elizabeth and I drove to Exmouth
for a weekend Christian conference. During the Saturday
evening session, the head pains returned to me in their
full violence, being particularly bad behind the right eye.
As the meeting ended, one of the ministering group
rose to say that he felt that there was someone present
who needed a physical healing from the Lord and would
that person come forward for prayer. I knew that this
meant me, but didn't move. The word was repeated,
and I realized that I must respond. Rising, I went to the
front and closed my eyes waiting for all that the Lord
had for me. After a few moments I looked around and
was surprised to see Elizabeth by my side and another
dozen people standing across the front of the meeting.

Two men came to pray with us. I knew them well: one
had become a Christian in my own living room. They
didn't question our presence but prayed for everything

that came to mind — our family, our relationship, our home, our ministry — it was a beautiful prayer that didn't even mention my reason for being there. As they moved on, I waited to catch their attention so that they would learn of my real need and pray again, but failed so to do.

It was then that I became aware of something happening in my body. On the crown of my head and to the right-hand side I felt a pin-point of intense cold. Slowly and beneath my scalp the pin-point extended into a line across the top of my skull to the right-hand side of my forehead traversing to the eye-socket. In another minute the line of cold emerged from the other side of the eye-socket, moving towards the bridge of my nose. For about two minutes I knew of this sharply defined line of cold, then it dissipated.

Thoughtfully I returned to my room, sharing this strange experience with Elizabeth. She encouraged me to believe that the Lord had healed me. Be that as it may, there had to be an explanation for the clearly observed physical event of which I was the sole witness. I woke next morning and my thoughts again centred on what had happened. I couldn't approach the matter from a medical viewpoint for I knew nothing of medicine: I could however look at it as a process of physics. If a fracture repaired, I mused, new bone must form along the fracture line to bond the breakage. If bone was created it seemed to me that energy would be absorbed. That being the case, the temperature locally would fall. Such a temperature change would, however, not be noticed in a body where the process occurred slowly, the blood circulation washing out the effect. If then the natural process of fracture mending in the body was energy-consumptive — and for me it had happened over a couple of minutes — then it seemed that I had actually witnessed the healing of my own fractured skull.

Going to breakfast, I met a young lady who was entering medical training and with whom in the past I had had many discussions of a scientific bent.

'Cindy,' I said, 'tell me, when a bone heals, is the process energy-consumptive or energy-productive?'

Slowly, she worked her way through the identical path of reasoning that I had traversed, 'It consumes energy: the process is energy-consumptive,' she concluded.

With a mixture of joy and awe in my heart I realized that just as the Lord had taken me along a path, using the sort of logic with which I was comfortable, to a point of faith in the whole of the Bible as authoritative and accurate, so he had now allowed me to use, on this occasion, the same faculty to discern his healing hand at work in my own body. In both cases the very things that would seem to confound scientific reasoning were in fact underwritten by scientific principles. While my Christian life was to be walked in faith — and that faith was to be in God and not my intellectual and scientific grasp of facts — by faith I would understand and that understanding did not necessarily negate the fundamentals of my own training.

10

The Car Crash

Because of an engineering training I suppose that it was a natural thing for me to be interested in motor cars. From the moment that I owned my first car, a 1933 Riley, they accumulated around me and dominated my life. Bits that weren't actually attached to wheels soon filled every available corner and by the time that I became a Christian, the driveway was the depository for five cars, the garage was filled with spare parts and the house contained all the cleaner bits. Elizabeth, who had no interest in mechanics at all, was indoctrinated to the point that she could eventually recognize the sound of a loose tappet or a melted 'big-end' bearing.

In the heady months after that initial meeting with the Lord I became progressively less easy about this consuming hobby that filled every moment of my life, yet I was reconciled to it because there was a useful product, a motor car. Vintage cars were, however, a passion that I would let go only slowly and in any case, cars were yet to play a part in the events of my life.

Elizabeth and I had been Christians for about five months when we took the holiday in Exmoor that led to my first preaching engagement. The car we had used for the occasion was a 1936 Riley which cruised very happily at 55 m.p.h. but which lost comfort at any other speed. We had planned to return from that holiday via Bristol and the road that we chose took us to Bridgwater northwards to Bristol. This road, the A38, had a very straight portion, miles in length, going across a flat, low-lying plain towards the foot of the Mendip Hills. It was a three-lane highway, one for northbound traffic and one for southbound, while the centre-lane was for overtaking. We were a mile or so north of Burnham-on-Sea when we drew behind a northbound queue of vehicles, maybe up to a dozen cars, travelling at 50 m.p.h. Nothing was on either the southbound or the centre-lane, so at a speed differential of 5 m.p.h. I pulled out to the centre-lane and began passing. It was a slow process and, after a short while, I noticed in the distance a line of vehicles coming south off the hills a mile or so away. From the back of this line there drew out onto the centre-lane a white car which began to pass the southbound line. Both our vehicles were now on the passing lane, travelling in the opposite direction and, though we were still a long way apart, our closing speed was possibly about 120 m.p.h. As we rapidly drew closer, I realized that it would be more discreet to pull into the northbound lane but, since I was rather more than half-way along the northbound line of vehicles running nose to tail, this proved impossible. The only thing to do was to brake, pulling behind all the cars I had just passed. The driver of the white car also had the same problem and it took me not long to realize that we were committed to a head-on collision, neither of us being able to pull out of the centre-lane and neither, in the space available, being able to stop.

The only action that I could countenance was to brake as hard as possible, at least to reduce the severity of the impact. Elizabeth had watched the rapidly developing crisis and, realizing what was about to happen, did the one thing that a Christian can do. She shouted 'Jesus.'

Now the same word can be used as an expletive or as a prayer, depending upon the attitude of the heart from which it comes: for Elizabeth, this was a cry from the heart for the Lord Jesus to intervene. He did! We were no more than six cars' lengths apart when, on the southbound lane, where there had a moment before been nose-to-tail traffic, there was a gap about the length of a car: one instant it was not there and the next, it was. The driver of the southbound white car saw the gap and with

a violent movement of his steering wheel pulled into it
so that we missed each other by no more than inches.
His startled, ashen face and his frightened, wide-open
eyes, remain imprinted upon my memory — but so does
the amazement at the miracle we saw that ensured our
safety. We continued our journey in safety, shaken, but
thanking the Lord for his protecting hand. It had been
astonishing to see the gap in the traffic where there was
no gap and, were we not rather numb from the shock of
the near-hit, we would have been quite overawed during
that moment.

★   ★   ★

We tend to think that when the Lord acts in a particular
way in a situation, he will repeat himself as the situation
is repeated. This, we were to learn, is not so — and just
as well since, if it were, the whole of the Christian life
would be reduced to a series of conditioned reflexes. As
it is, we need to keep a contact, in any set of circumstances, with the Lord God to know his will. It took a
long time to learn that and, in reality, it is still brought to
us both as a principle and as an application, such is our
human tendency to want everything to operate in pre-
dictable paths.

A Jaguar had replaced the Rileys as daily transport by
the time, some years later, that we had arranged to spend
a day with a couple who were old friends and lived about
forty miles from our home. The husband and I had
been students together, when we did all the things that
students tend to do. As a drinking buddy I had found
agreement with his atheistic stand, which John was prepared to express strongly. Such had been our friendship
that Elizabeth and I had been among the small group of
friends who had attended his marriage to Gwyneth
where we had acted both as witnesses and then as cour-
iers of the news of the wedding to their unsuspecting
families. The friendship had continued, but now Elizabeth and I were Christians — a threat to any friendship
with atheists.

Before setting out on our day's visit we had prayed much for John and Gwyneth. How we longed that they and our other old friends would come to know the Lord as we had. In the first year or so of our Christian lives we had prayed for an opportunity to speak to other friends and the opportunity had always occurred: now, as we prayed, there was confidence that there would be the moment when we could break the news, but also the sense of trepidation at the way in which my friend would dispose of my statements, intellectually and technically weak by the standards of many earlier conversations.

That English summer had produced a six-week drought and much rubber and grease from vehicles had accumulated on the road surfaces. Shortly before we set out, on the morning of our visit, there had been a very heavy rainstorm and the combination of water, grease and rubber on the roads made them rather slippery. We had a choice of route, fast or picturesque, and chose the latter which took us through pleasant hills and woodland. The car was running well, the exhaust crackling on the over-run as we topped the hills and geared down for the corners before accelerating through them, the tail of the car hanging slightly out with modest oversteer. It was all that pleasant motoring was meant to be about!

I didn't notice the road-sign to warn of the bend in the road towards the edge of the wood: bushes had grown across it. The curve was masked to my view by the arrangement of the trees and it tightened up rapidly as I pulled the car into it, realizing that my speed was rather high. There was no way of knowing that the surface camber of the road became adverse in the corner just where the tree droppings added to the wet, oily surface.

The steering went light in my hand as the front wheels lost their adhesion and I realized, as the nose of the car began to swing wide, that it was understeering. There was not enough width in the road to accelerate the engine, pulling the rear wheels out and I knew that braking was out of the question: all that could be done was to put on more lock. Its effectiveness was nil.

As we crossed the central line of the road, the truck

came from the other direction. It was a ten-ton model travelling briskly into the corner from a long straight road: it was green, large and right in our path. My Jaguar hit it head-on.

As a student I had been in a car-crash late one night after the Varsity rugby match. I had been the front-seat passenger in a car that was hit sideways on and I recall being thrown from the vehicle and feeling the wheels of the other car brush past my head. I'd been a bit shaken but little else had stayed with me as a memory. On this occasion the overriding memory is that of the speed of events and the noise of the impact: I had never in my life heard anything as loud. The Jaguar spun away down the road being hit in the side by a further vehicle and the eerie silence that ensued was even more dramatic after the noise of the impact.

Deeply shaken, I turned to Elizabeth to speak, but she was not there: her seat was empty. Slowly it entered my dazed mind that the bundle rolled up in the front foot-well under the dashboard was the still body of my wife. She didn't respond as I spoke and seeing her face with eyes closed I recall the look of serene peace upon her. Turning in my seat I addressed Matthew, but he wasn't in his place either, nor was he in the foot-well. Confused, I looked around the cockpit of the car only to realize slowly that Elizabeth's door was wide open. As my eyes took me through the opened door they focused upon a leg that I recognized to be Matthew's, extending from beneath the car. From its position it was evident that Matthew's body was beneath the car and, as the car had spun, I had run over him. Rachel was the other occupant of the car and had been sat immediately behind me. I strained in the seat harness to see if she was all right. It happened that just before the impact she had picked up a large teddy-bear which, held in front of her, had been an effective cushion. She was in her seat and conscious but in the drama of the moment was looking for the comfort of her father. What she saw as I turned was totally unexpected and, for my part, I couldn't understand the look of horror on her face as she began to weep. Instead of her father's normal face, she saw what I was not yet aware of — deep lacerations going centrally up my nose and across my forehead with blood pouring out.

It was then that, in the comparative silence, I heard a noise upon which my ears hadn't previously focused: fuel from the tank which had been filled just a few miles before, was pumping out on the engine and the road. As an engineer I knew that with a hot engine and loose fuel there was a high likelihood of an explosion and fire at any moment and the only thing to do was to get my family and myself away from the wreckage quickly. But there were problems. The doors on the driver's side of the car would not open, for they had been hit by the third vehicle: there was no room for me to move as I discovered that I was pinned to my seat by the steering-wheel and column which was against my chest: I couldn't move my legs since the whole of the dashboard had come into the passenger compartment with the engine — and my legs were under the twisted pile of metal, wood and instruments. I was trapped and I knew it. My daughter was crying quietly, unable to move from her seat, Matthew lay apparently dead beneath the wheels of my own car while Elizabeth's inert body told me that she must be dead also.

It was a moment of unbelievable horror to realize what I had done — and that can be relived even in writing this — and now I waited to die, thinking that the incident might merit a small mention in the national newscast on radio that night. Yet, in that moment of extremity, something totally unpremeditated and thus unexpected, happened. Without calling upon the name of the Lord or crying to God in any way, I suddenly was aware of his presence. In the cold, analytical climate of my normal world, it is impossible to quantify that knowledge of his presence or even adequately to describe it: all that can be said was that I knew he was there; seated in the wreck with us. My natural self wanted to scream at the prospect that I had killed two members of my own family and that the remaining member was about to perish with me in the inevitable holocaust, but that reaction was entirely

negated by the overwhelming sense of peace in the assurance that he was there. Disaster was around me and
death was before me, but from that standpoint of peace
it no longer seemed to matter, since I was aware that the
God who was there was in control of the situation. It
didn't make sense in rational terms, but I knew that, of
the horror I had created, the outcome, whatever it may
be, was under his control and thus in his will. If I died
with my family, so be it: the Lord had made the decision
that this was my time. If I lived, so be it, he had a plan as
yet to be worked out.

My attention turned to a stranger at the window of the
driver's door — an ambulance had been called but could
he make a phone call on my behalf? I gave him my
address book which was on hand and asked him to call
John and, without mentioning the car crash, say simply
that we wouldn't be meeting them. Meanwhile, hands
were grasping at Rachel to get her out of the car, others
were gently pulling Matthew's body from beneath it and
then I drew the rescuer's attention to Elizabeth's body
in the front foot-well. Finally hands were pulling at me
and I was hauled unceremoniously from the wreckage,
legs following helplessly as they were disengaged from
the remains of the front of the car.

We were all lined up on the grassy bank when Elizabeth
showed signs of movement and soon after that, Matthew
regained consciousness. Two ambulances arrived, one
of which had actually been on another call and was only
a short distance away when it was redirected to the accident. We were piled onto stretchers and whisked away
to the Lister Hospital in Hitchin. As we were borne along
the road, the sirens of the two ambulances sounding
strangely distant, we could not have known that we were
entering a period in which we were to see the miraculous
hand of God at work.

★   ★   ★

John had been telephoned by the anonymous helper
who had told him that we had been in a terrible accident

and were on our way to the hospital in Hitchin. Alarmed, John had leapt into his car arriving only shortly after we had at the Emergency Admissions Department. He entered to find the whole Peacock family lying on stretchers and he looked as if he was going to weep. He and I talked sporadically as, one by one, the family was taken through an opening into an examination room before being despatched to various wards in the building. Elizabeth had a fractured leg, but her head had taken a beating and was beginning to show it. One tooth from the upper jaw was missing and a second was hanging loose. Matthew, miraculously, appeared to have no broken bones and there were no wheel marks on him at all. He did however have a badly scored hip. Rachel's only evident problem was a blood-blister under a bruised little-fingernail and in due course the nail was lost before a replacement grew. It was only later that we became aware of the psychological damage as, rapidly, the hair of this eight-year-old turned white. For my part, the damage was suspected multiple fractures in both legs — it turned out that neither was broken — and the need for stitches all the way up my nose and across my forehead.

In my examination I was laid out just inside the opening to the room and the doctor, an Indian lady, who had already attended to my family, dealt with me. In attendance there was also a nurse, making a record of all my personal details. As the stitches began to go in I was asked my name, address, age, name of family doctor, next of kin, and my religion.

The last question woke me up and I responded, 'Yes.'

'But what is your religion?' I was asked.

'I'm a Christian, what are you?' was my reply. The young nurse looked embarrassed, so I redirected the question at my attentive doctor.

'I am nothing,' the doctor replied. 'I have tried all religions and none of them mean anything.'

Before me was a captive audience: the doctor couldn't escape for she had to sew me up and the nurse had to attend the presence of the doctor, so I replied boldly,

'What a pity, for you've never met Jesus.' That sparked off a discussion by the end of which the doctor, who was in England for just one week, agreed to accept the gift of a Gideons Bible with which she was presented a couple of days later. I thought that I had been witnessing to two people, oblivious of the fact that just behind my head was an open door on the other side of which, less than eighteen inches from my head, was my atheist friend John, also listening.

As I was discharged that day, I visited Elizabeth, lying quite stunned in a hospital bed, her face rapidly becoming discoloured and swollen as the bruising worked its way out. She gave me instructions to bring a suitcase of her personal things from home, told me that she was being visited the next day by the dentist who was going to remove the loose tooth and then pointed at the window opposite her bed.

'I've been trying to think where I've seen a window like that before,' she said, 'and I recall it's what I saw in the vision that the Lord gave me last evening.'

The previous evening seemed an eternity away but, casting my mind back, I remembered Elizabeth seemed slightly disturbed after a time of private prayer.

She had told me, 'The Lord gave me a vision of a single-storey house with a veranda outside. The roof of the building stretched across the veranda and was supported with columns which carried climbing flowers. There were windows in the wall under the veranda. When I asked the Lord to speak to tell me what this meant,' she said, 'he gave me a scripture in the Psalms, "For in the time of trouble he shall hide me in his pavilion: in the secret of his tabernacle shall he hide me." Roy, I think that we are going to move house.'

Now, though, she was saying that perhaps the Lord was warning us of the problem of the coming day — certainly the window with the glazing bars running horizontally and vertically matched the vision.

John was a tremendous help: he abandoned his diary and became my chauffeur as, painfully, I moved from one necessary job to the next, and, following our dis-

charge from hospital, his home became a sort of field
hospital for Rachel and me since we were quite in-
capable of caring for ourselves. One of the first things
for me to do was to buy a pair of dark spectacles, for by
the morning after the crash the front of my face had
become so swollen that, with two amazing black eyes
also, I couldn't be recognized. I decided that it was
better to look like an out-of-work actor than the prize-
fighter who lost. A chemist shop thus became my first
priority the next day but, as I entered, I was greeted by
the startled gaze of the chemist.

'Goodness, what on earth have you been up to?' he
exclaimed.

'Oh, I had a head-on argument with a ten-ton truck.'

'Yes, I can see that. The skin is healing up beautifully,'
he continued, examining the front of my face closely.
'That happened about five days ago?'

'As a matter of fact, I was lying in the wreckage of my
car less than twenty-four hours ago,' I told him.

'Impossible . . . skin just does not heal that quickly.
Those stitches though . . . that's the best stitchwork I've
ever seen.'

That observation was confirmed by my doctor and we
were to find out why it was so good. I later discovered
that the doctor who had stitched me up happened to be
one of India's leading plastic surgeons. She had just
completed a duty in the USA and was travelling back
to India, spending one week with friends in England
when she heard that the local hospital in Hitchin had a
desperate need over a period of a couple of days for a
doctor to deal with admissions. In this way, the Lord had
arranged for the best stitchcraft on the front of my face,
as a result of which I wouldn't spend the rest of my life
looking like a companion of Count Dracula!

After medical attention to his hip and detailed checks
for concussion effects, Matthew was released from hospital. Daily, Elizabeth showed signs of improvement as
she gave me regular reports of her treatment which always
included the statement that the dentist was going to remove the offending tooth the next day. While most

grateful that she was alive and delighted that when the bruises and swelling disappeared from her face she would again be looking like the girl I married, I was rather saddened that the removal of this tooth would leave an unsightly gap in her mouth. Elizabeth had always had rather crowded upper teeth, there being quite a bit of overlap, but that had been preferable to a wide space that would call for the wearing of dentures. The leg fracture was however doing well, there being no displacement of the bone sections.

Eventually the time came for her to be discharged and slowly we walked from the hospital, Elizabeth learning to use a pair of crutches. We had been a little surprised that her leg had not been put in a cast but she seemed to manage quite well without it. A few yards from the building in which she had been, Elizabeth paused to look at it: it was a single-storey building with a veranda whose roof, an extension from the main roof, was supported by columns carrying climbing plants. The wall of the building under the veranda had a series of windows with glazing bars of the type that she could see from her hospital bed. It was exactly as the vision that God had given her the day before the accident: in the day of trouble the Lord had been with us and he had hid us in his pavilion to save us from the death that had seemed inevitable.

My first anxiety upon getting Elizabeth home was to get attention for the tooth that still had not been dealt with by the hospital dentist. I telephoned our family dentist, but he was away on a week's holiday. His associate had a full appointments book and so I decided to take her to the local hospital in Bedford to get the extraction done immediately.

We drove the eight miles in a silence that was terminated by Elizabeth's comment, 'It's strange that there should be so much difficulty in getting this tooth taken out. I wonder if the Lord is saying something. Perhaps he doesn't want me to have it out.'

It was at the gate of the hospital that we turned the car around and drove back to Ampthill, wondering what was to happen.

For the remainder of the week the tooth continued to flap and upon his return the following Monday, Elizabeth was visiting Gordon, the dentist. He examined the tooth carefully and confirmed that the damage had killed the nerve.

'If I don't take it out,' he said, 'it will turn black and become very unsightly, so I should remove it immediately. However,' he continued, thoughtfully, 'I don't want to rush in where angels fear to tread — maybe God is doing something. I think that we'll leave it for three weeks and then I'll look at it again.'

Over those three weeks, Elizabeth and I watched, as, imperceptibly at first, the tooth moved sideways around the gum until it straddled the space covering its original position and that of the missing tooth. Then it moved back into line with the other teeth in the gum. When Gordon examined it, he was able to report that the tooth was now firmly set in the gum and that the nerve was alive. A year or so later Elizabeth and I were visiting a church in which we were sharing on the subject of 'Miracles Today'. Reference was made to the car crash and at the end of the meeting, Gordon, who was in the congregation, rose to share his own professional observations on Elizabeth's tooth, declaring that he had witnessed a miracle.

Rachel's hair became a concern for us and it wasn't long before in the blackboard jungle of school life she, going rapidly white, became the object of derision among her age group. We prayed much for her and over a long period of time saw her hair gently turning dark again. It had been explained to us that white hair does not regain its colour, but hers did. As this process slowly continued, it was possible to see individual hairs with the colour growing out of their roots towards the white ends. Today, Rachel has a thin and attractive silver line in a head of dark-brown hair, a feature that many think has been bleached in.

It was about a week and a half after the accident that we were booked to go to Lee Abbey as part of the Youth Camp team and it was there that we saw God using the incident for his purposes. As a subject for the epilogue one evening I was asked to relate what had happened in the car crash. The attention was intense as the story was unfolded and at the end of the meeting a challenge was made for those who didn't know the God who had been in the car with me, to meet him: about thirty-five did that evening.

The car in which we had gone to that camp had been very small and after the family had bundled in with all the odds and ends that camping demands, there was no way in which we could fit Elizabeth's crutches in.

She had been worried about how one could move around a camp field on crutches and a very young Rachel had remarked, 'I expect he'll tell you to leave them behind.'

'Who'll tell me to leave what behind?' asked her mother.

'Jesus will tell you to leave your crutches behind,' Rachel explained.

So it was, by the circumstances of the moment, that Elizabeth went to the camp with a broken leg, but with no cast and no crutches. Because it was a particularly muddy year, the Camp Director had insisted upon a walking stick being made available, but when, six weeks later Elizabeth presented herself at the hospital, she first had to learn to use the crutches. An astonished hospital staff couldn't understand why she had no leg cast, only to conclude that the two doctors involved had each thought the other had ordered the cast. Pleased with her progress though, they recommended that she should continue with the crutches, as before.

It was about three weeks after the accident that we were visited by Mark and Mavis whom we had known in Hemingford Grey. By now, my two black eyes had turned a very ripe purple-yellow and so had both Elizabeth's and Matthew's. My stitches had the usual congealed blood on them, Elizabeth was on her walking stick, Matthew was still moving slowly because of the hip bruising and Rachel's hand was plastered as the nail detached. Our visitors had known nothing of what had happened, so we presented an astonishing sight to them. I think that they had the impression we had had a really memorable family row, but upon explaining what had happened, Mavis asked when the crash had been. As I related to her the day and then, as she pressed further, the hour, she told us, 'That morning I was doing the washing-up in the kitchen, the children having gone to school and Mark having gone to the office, when the Lord clearly told me to pray for the Peacocks. I wiped my hands and walked into the sitting room, sat down and prayed for you, then returned to the kitchen. Immediately the Lord spoke to me again, "Pray for the Peacocks," so I went back into the sitting room and prayed about everything I could think of for you. When I got back into the kitchen the Lord spoke to me yet again and I said, "I don't know what to pray for," but this would not leave me, so I gave up my work for the morning and knowing of nothing else to do, I spent the whole time praying in tongues for you.'

Only then did we realize that, as we had lain injured and helpless in the wreck of that car, someone, under the direction of the Lord, had been praying for us throughout. In the day of trouble he was certainly arranging to guard us.

11

Weather Watch

Of course I'd read about it in the Bible — Jesus had stilled the storm, Elijah's word had altered the weather patterns in the land of Israel, the sun had even stood still on two occasions — but that was in the Bible. I was a scientist and, although not a meteorologist, was aware that it was quite out of the question to expect God to do anything about the weather. It was certainly within my experience by now that God in Jesus Christ had come to meet with men and that, by relating himself with men, was able to change their lives, but that had to represent a limit to the supernatural activity we might expect to find. Yet a series of events was to disturb that idea and remove it from the canon of rationalism that still wanted to dictate what God could and could not do.

Our awareness of the Lord's working in this area began with an open-air concert we had arranged in Bedfordshire. It was the height of summer and the height of the open-air music festivals: if the world's music could attract people to a festival we reasoned that Christian music should also do so and after prayer we felt that we were being led to have our own festival. It was arranged to be at a farm in the middle of the county and we secured the services of Merv and Merla, two singers whose ministry was much used. Posters and handbills were prepared and while some of the handbills were distributed in advance, a large number were kept back for distribution in the local villages on the day of the event.

The day dawned and an anxious look through the

bedroom curtains confirmed my worst fears: a leaden sky was yielding a steady downpour of rain.

In mid-morning the team of handbill distributors began to arrive and, by the car-load, I handed them over, hands filled with wet bills at various points around the county. Returning from pushing the last group out into the rain, I drove to the back of the house and made to enter by the back door. As I pushed at it, I found that the door into the kitchen would only open an inch or so before it jammed against a solid object. Walking outside, I looked enquiringly into the window of the large kitchen and my eyes met an astonishing sight. All of the furniture in the room had been cleared out and the whole floor area was jammed with the bodies of young people kneeling in prayer. Through the rain channelling down the window-pane as I stood soaking in the heavy fall, I saw with horror that they were asking the Lord God to stop the rain. My immediate and main concern was for the inevitable disappointment and damage to their faith when the rain, which was evidently set for the day, continued unabated.

That, though, would not have been the concern uppermost in my mind had I been aware of the location of Merv and Merla. I thought that they were somewhere in England, not knowing that in fact they had woken up that morning in Brussels, Belgium. As they rose, they too had been greeted with heavy rain, and had set out on their journey to the meeting, their car ploughing through the weather. They drove south into northern France towards the Boulogne ferry, the rain continuing as heavily. They crossed the English Channel to Dover in heavy rain which continued as they drove through Canterbury to London and then north along the M1 motorway to Bedfordshire. They left the motorway at Junction 12, the rain continuing as heavily as before, but as they approached Ampthill they noticed that the weather was changing to a drizzle while, not far away to their right, they saw a break in the clouds.

In Ampthill we found that the rain was easing at lunch-time and, by the time that the singers had arrived, it had ceased altogether. A little to the east we could see a break in the clouds and, arriving in Maulden, the village to the east where the meeting was to be held, we found that the sun had broken through. We drove our cars to the field where a stage had been set on a large hay-wain and, passing through the gate, walked on dry, firm ground to the stage. As people began to arrive, the ground around the gateway remained firm and in fact over the whole of the afternoon it was never reduced to mud in spite of both the earlier rain and the heavy traffic.

Through the afternoon the sun shone down upon us, yet in any direction that we cared to look, there were storm clouds above the near horizons. The concert finished without one spot of rain having descended, yet the national evening news contained many reports of bad weather and promises that the uniform wetness over the United Kingdom would continue without change. My mind went back to that moment with the sight of all those young people praying for the Lord to stop the rain. I realized that their prayer had been answered in quite a dramatic way by the Lord who had shown in the Bible that he was able to do it.

★   ★   ★

We were to find that the Lord was able to use weather patterns for many purposes. It was only one day later that, as a family, we set off for a month's Christian work in southern France. Our purpose was to join a group of Christians, mainly American, constructing a large camp site for Christian use. It was set in the mountains of the Massif Central overlooking the Rhône valley about ninety kilometres north of Marseilles.

Our earlier disastrous experience in camping was leading us to undertake more preparation on this occasion and, since we now had a large station wagon with a huge roof-rack, we used all the space we could to transport all the artefacts of a civilized lifestyle with us. We had no less than three large tents, an igloo-type structure as a bedroom for Elizabeth and me, a frame-tent for the children to sleep in and a ridge-tent to be used as a kitchen. Every tent was spacious and with the generally excellent weather and unbelievably cheap fruit, we had all the elements of a good holiday.

It wasn't just for a holiday that we were there, though — work was to be done and over the month I was involved in framing a house and digging a septic tank large enough to serve an army. Progress was slow: we rose early before the sun's heat was too intense and my first job of the day was to lead a Bible study through David, an American, who acted as interpreter. Daily, an hour's work was done before a break for a cold drink and soon I noticed that very little more was attempted during the day: both the French-speaking and English-speaking members of the team were becoming progressively idle.

Although we enjoyed remarkable weather during the daytime, we had been at the camp site only a week or so when the nights were disturbed by distant thunderstorms in the mountains. Eventually a storm settled, one night, over our mountain. Our children, who were still quite small, had been put to bed and we had retired, when we were woken by a flash of lightning and the roar of thunder. Like most people I had been in many thunderstorms, but never before had I experienced one while in a tent. It was at first fascinating to see the tent illuminated by the momentary light penetrating the walls but then, as the centre of the storm became closer and more intense, it became rather frightening.

Since the lightning was having such an effect upon us, I reasoned that the children were also frightened and decided to go to them. It was raining as I fumbled with the zip-fastener of their tent and crawled in, only to find them sleeping deeply. Since the storm showed no signs of abating, I decided to sit with them and did so for about half an hour as the storm raged about us.

By now I had become used to it, but my reverie was disturbed as I saw the tent zipper being slowly opened.

Elizabeth's pale face looked through the gap as she said, 'Roy, our air beds are afloat: there's a flood running right through our tent.' The night was becoming a night-mare so we decided to evacuate, moving to a barn, occupied by David and another young man, and attached to a farmhouse thirty yards away. For some reason French barns seem to have the door half-way up the wall and can only be entered by a ladder, so with one child wrapped in a sleeping bag and over my shoulder, I climbed the ladder and beat upon the door. Eventually the occupants woke up and let us in. I returned with Elizabeth and another child and, feeling like refugees, we decided to stay in the barn for the remainder of the night.

The floor was hard and so I returned to our flooded tents to collect beds and bedding. I went first to the igloo tent, but, climbing through the small entrance, inadvertently knocked the top off the portable gas light I was carrying. I had done this before and burnt my hand trying to replace the hot part, so this time took great care. Sat on my haunches I was gingerly edging the top of the gas light back into place when suddenly the tips of my fingers touching the metal parts registered a sharp, extreme pain. At the same moment, the pain was repeated at every joint in my body — fingers, wrists, elbows, ankles and feet. It was violent and I felt as if I had been put on a high-speed rack for stretching. I stumbled back with the shock, and shock it was, for as my disorientated thoughts were organized, I realized that there was a roar of thunder in my ears and I had seen a large flash. I had been struck by lightning — and I had lived.

That I was very frightened is an understatement. I was alive but what would happen if there was a second strike? Wasn't it more likely for a second discharge to follow the ionized path left by the first? Trying to steady and reassure myself I recalled the adage that lightning does not strike in the same place twice. It was repeated several times over in my mind but I felt neither steadied nor reassured. Then I remembered that in times of crisis, Christians should pray, so I did that and have to confess that I didn't feel much better after that either.

Crawling out of the tent I hurried back towards the

barn and, glancing up to the sky, saw an amazing and awesome sight: the whole of the heavens above me were illuminated with the changing tracery of lightning moving among the clouds. I was filled with an awe of God at that moment — an awe that has remained with me since then. As I approached the barn I was greeted by the wavering voice of David calling from the doorway of the barn, 'Roy, don't touch the metal ladder if you see lightning coming this way.'

Ignoring the fact that lightning travels at the speed of light — a little faster than I could move anyway — I looked over my shoulder to see if there was any lightning coming this way. Getting into the barn, I was greeted by Elizabeth and David with a most remarkable story. While I had been in my tent, the deteriorating weather had prompted David to invite some other people, also camping, to shelter in the barn. Leaning out of the barn door and supporting himself on the top of the steel ladder, he was calling to their tent when the lightning struck.

Elizabeth described it: 'One moment David was standing right by me, then he wasn't. I heard a thump at the far wall and saw David hitting the wall about six feet up, then collapsing in a heap on the floor.'

The lightning strike had then also touched the ladder, hurling David about thirty feet, but leaving my wife completely untouched.

The next morning we gathered as a rather frightened group for our Bible study. There had been surprisingly little physical damage: the porcelain fuses had been blown out of the uncovered fuse-box in the farmhouse and had shattered against the opposite wall of the room, but little else was damaged except our nerves. We began to examine what the Lord may have been saying to us — reproving us for our dilatory behaviour — when David, the interpreter, began to weep under conviction.

Eventually, he and I withdrew to be alone together when I said, 'David, I recall reading in a magazine a few years ago about your ordination at Bible College. The memorable feature, as I remember, was that when hands were laid on you, there was a lightning flash and

thunderclap which was interpreted as a sign of the hand
of God on you. Why is it that on that occasion he showed
his approbation, but this time he knocked you over?'

David, in tears, then told me of a totally wrong relationship with a girl, determined to get the matter right
immediately — and did just that.

As we all returned to the work for which we had been
called in France, it was with a sense that the Lord had
used the weather in a most unusual way to speak to us,
revealing his glory, his majesty and the seriousness of
the calling upon our lives. The Christian life was not
going to be a game or even a hobby that we could take
up or put down as we wished: it was to be a serious
response to the most serious call that could be placed
upon a person's life.

In England, where twenty minutes without any rain is
normally greeted with alarm by farmers, 1976 was the
year of the great drought. It was also the year of our
second visit to the Lee Abbey camp. Instead of the wallow-
ing mud of the first visit we were in glorious sunshine on
a sun-baked field overshadowed by the thick forest that
spilled over from Woody Bay, the next bay south. As
before, one of my jobs was to speak at three or four of
the epilogues on a series of predetermined subjects.

One evening about half-way through the two-week
period I was to speak on the subject of 'Prayer' and so
shared enthusiastically about the privilege and joy of
prayer and the answers to prayer that we may expect. It
was a windy evening with the wind in an unusual quarter
that disturbed the canvas of the marquee, making it
difficult to be heard without the help of a microphone.
As I was finishing my address, a note was handed to me.
It read:

> Please announce that there is a forest fire in Woody Bay
> and it is being blown in this direction. If it continues at the
> present rate the camp will have to be evacuated at 2 a.m.
> Girls must go to the house (on the other side of the valley)

and boys must act as beaters and move equipment.

I read it out and couldn't help but notice the sharp contrast between the victorious statements of my positive message: 'the prayer in our extremity is God's opportunity to do the miracle', and the defeat in reading this note.

Perhaps the Lord was calling us to put the word into practice and our faith on the line and so with much fear in my heart, I asked the audience of one hundred and twenty young people to bow their heads. Referring to the message shared I asked, 'How many believe that the Lord God can put out the forest fire? If you do, I want you to indicate that to me by raising your hand. If you don't, don't raise your hand. But before anyone responds, remember this: yours may be the only hand in this marquee that goes up. If that is the case, a great deal depends upon your prayer alone. Now, without looking around, indicate to me.'

I was overwhelmed as a sea of hands was raised and glancing about felt that I could see no more than one person without a hand held up. It was with a terrible sense of responsibility that I led the short prayer, unambiguously worded, in which we called upon the Lord to put out the fire. As I was praying aloud I noticed that my voice was carrying much better, for the background noise of the flapping marquee canvas was dying away: the wind was falling in that moment.

The meeting dispersed and Mike, one of the older team members told me, 'I walked to the top of the hill that overlooks Woody Bay and, before me I saw the forest fire blazing. Over the next fifteen minutes though, the appearance was almost as if it was being sprayed with a giant aerosol, for the flames simply died out until there was no fire to be seen.'

The wind which had been blowing the fire towards the camp had dropped, even as we were praying, and the Lord had completed the work by putting out the fire in a further quarter of an hour or so. We had much for which to thank the Lord, not least of which was that we had been observers of a miracle and had the privilege of partaking in the prayer that led to it: at the time, I must say, our main cause for thanking the Lord seemed to be that we were not called upon to get up at two o'clock in the morning.

The scientist in me had not wanted to concede that weather patterns, large-scale effects apparently random in nature, which in general didn't seem to have anything to do with the spiritual lives of people, could be under the control of God. I had to admit, though, that the prayers the young people had demonstrated before me in the kitchen and the prayer in the marquee at Lee Abbey, had been followed by abrupt changes that did not seem to have a logical explanation. Could chance have governed those situations — a small sun-lit hole in an overcast sky and that hole right over the group of fields that we used for our concert and the wind dropping at the instant we were praying in the youth camp? If that was chance, albeit with enormous and unfathomable odds against it happening, how had the forest fire gone out in fifteen minutes and then how was it, that, out of all the people on the mountain top in France at that moment of the lightning strike (about twelve of us), it was David who was thrown over? If I had to apply a scientific judgement to such a complex series of events, I would have to do so in statistical terms. If all these things could be explained in terms of probability, then the science of statistical analysis was crazy. My only viable explanation was that the Lord who had called me into a serious relationship with himself was in control — and was letting me see it.

12

The Upper Room

Our arrival in Ampthill had not been auspicious; no gas, no electricity, no water and even no floor in one room. In the coldest part of winter we soon assumed a siege mentality, trying to deal with the crisis of the moment: Elizabeth was attempting to run a kitchen that had been badly designed three hundred years before and hadn't improved with age, while I was rather like the old woman discovered by King Wenceslas — continually looking for pieces of wood to keep a fire going. Ours was not the smooth transition into a new social scene, although a local newspaper was moved to devote an article to our arrival with the headline 'Roy likes Cars, Clocks and God': for us there was a fight to exist. Because of the adverse circumstances we were forced to ask ourselves several times whether we were out of the will of God in being there. Was this attempt to follow the Lord a huge mistake? Every time, we went back to the series of words to which we had attempted to be obedient, but we couldn't see where we had gone wrong. Further, there had been a prophecy during one of Dick Carter's visits that the glory we had seen at the early meetings in our home in Derby was nothing compared with the glory we would yet see. If that was the case, why was everything going wrong? Perhaps after all, the whole thing was hocus-pocus: there was no God and somehow we now had to dig ourselves out of the hole into which we had got ourselves.

We were not then in a position to welcome guests either for physical comfort or spiritual fellowship when

the door bell rang a couple of Thursday nights after our
arrival. Three men stood at the door, Eric, Leslie and
Horace, each with a Bible under his arm. 'We've come to
have fellowship with you,' they said. I felt a little like
Abraham at the door of his tent when he saw the three
men. For us it was certainly fellowship that these men
brought and it did us good, so it was with some joy that
we heard the door bell ring on the following Thursday
evening. A small group of Christians stood there: they
too had arrived for fellowship — and this continued for
the next week and the next. Within two months there
was a regular group coming every Thursday, just as had
happened in Derby.

The numbers fluctuated as the years went by, going as
high as about one hundred and sixty on one occasion,
but there usually seemed to be a core group of between
thirty and forty present. We never knew where they
came from, that was not our business, nor was their
denominational colour of any interest. We didn't invite
anyone, but somehow they came. Mostly they were
people who were hungry for more of Christ, a few were
curious and only once or twice did anyone come to criticize.

Why God had drawn us into these meetings was difficult to know at first: we realized that we weren't meant
to be a church as the word is normally used, but our
terms of reference were well stated by someone who
described the meetings as a 'water-hole in the desert.'
The analogy was good: some people attended for a few
weeks and some for a few years and, having obtained
from God what they had come for, continued on their
way.

There were some events that were used of the Lord to
characterize the meetings that included prayer, praise
and a teaching from the Bible. One of the earlier memories followed an evening when Mark, who had been
converted in our home in Hemingford Grey and was
now in full-time Christian ministry, had been speaking.
There had been a good number of people present,
among whom was Sandra, a lady from an adjoining village. While he was staying at our house, Mark offered to

help me do a small construction job in the kitchen.

On the day following the meeting we began by mixing concrete to lay a plinth for some kitchen furniture. The mix was just about ready for pouring and the shuttering was already in place when the front-door bell rang. Sandra was at the door, asking if she could come in. I explained that Mark's wife and my wife were out but she insisted upon talking to us and then explained her mission. She reminded me that a couple of years before she had asked me to pray for a pain in her back. The pain had gone but had, to her surprise and discomfort, returned in a much aggravated manner a couple of days before. While travelling to the meeting on the previous evening she had asked the Lord if he would heal her at the meeting and, as a sign that he would, would he give a word of knowledge to someone present about her condition. The Lord had spoken to her, reminding her that, as a Christian she could go to the elders and ask for the laying-on of hands with prayer. She added that, in spite of the word from the Lord, she hadn't asked for prayer and now she was in acute pain — could we pray for her?

'Come along in and sit down,' she was told and then Mark took over the discussion.

'Do you happen to have one leg shorter than the other?' he asked and she, evidently surprised by the question, replied that she didn't know.

'Then we will measure your legs,' said Mark with authority, 'sit on this hard chair with your back pressed against the support and lift your legs to the horizontal.'

This done, Mark looked closely at her ankle bones, then with a note of triumph exclaimed, 'You see, brother Roy, the right leg is about seven-eighths of an inch shorter than the left.'

'Right,' he continued as he addressed Sandra, 'this is what we will do. Roy and I will pray for you — and the Lord will grow your leg — and you have to do nothing.'

'What nonsense is this?' I thought to myself. 'It is ludicrous to expect anything to happen.'

Nevertheless I felt that I should comply with this enthusiast who had evidently become quite mad in the last few moments. So Sandra held her legs in a horizontal attitude, Mark prayed and I, not being sure of the correct way of going about matters, closed my eyes, wringing my hands together.

'Thank you Jesus, thank you Lord,' Mark repeated several times and after a suitable length of time I opened my eyes to view progress. The right leg now seemed even shorter than it was before and the thought crossed my mind that perhaps we ought to stop praying before we had a real disaster on our hands. Standing there with eyes closed had been a singularly unprofitable exercise so I decided to watch what, if anything, was likely to happen. As I did, my eyes opened wide in astonishment and the note of Mark's voice changed to one of jubilation as I watched the short leg grow, over a period of three to four seconds, until the ankle bones of both legs were at the same level.

I was speechless, then very excited. What I had seen transcended any scientific explanation that I could offer; there could not have been a twisting of the hips or a natural moving of the legs one to another. There could be no doubt that I had seen a physical miracle of significant proportions and the evidence was before me.

Sandra left the house with a huge smile on her face and, I understand, has never had a recurrence of the back problem. Shortly after a hurried laying of the concrete which had waited in a liquid state for us, I too left the house on an errand. In the street I met Eric and with great excitement, told him what I had seen.

He, I knew, was to be speaking in a local church that evening so, as I completed my story I said, 'I wish I was to be in the pulpit instead of you — I think I'd lift the roof off the church!'

'It would be of no use,' Eric replied drily, 'they wouldn't believe you.'

I stumped down the street, this gold nugget of knowledge bursting to get out of me, when I espied my next victim, a Christian lady who had often been to the meetings at our home. After greeting her, the news spilled out of me in an excited flow.

As I finished, my unconcealed joy was shattered as she looked at me coldly and said, 'I don't believe you.'

'But you know me, I wouldn't lie to you — you've been to meetings in our home — do they encourage you to believe that I would lie?'

'The fact remains that I don't believe you,' was her only response. So Eric was right: it was no use telling people of the miracles, for even Christians wouldn't believe.

The scientist, though, is never slow to talk about any discovery he has made and I still longed to share this remarkable incident with others. Thursday night would be the ideal time, I schemed: at least I would be among people I knew and whose hearts may be open. I was not to know what Thursday night would bring.

It was a smallish group that gathered that evening, perhaps twenty, and the meeting progressed in a smooth way until I could hold back no longer. Again the news spilled out of me, but I was a little more wary on this occasion.

As I finished the story, the silence was broken by Ray, 'It happens that I have one leg shorter than the other. Perhaps I could have prayer for it?'

It was a heart-stopping moment, but as I looked at him, I knew that he was serious. But Ray was an Anglican priest connected with a local church. All eyes were now on me for I was the only person in the room who had seen a leg grow, so I was viewed as the specialist! What would Mark have done in the circumstance? Oh yes, I could remember.

'Perhaps we could measure your legs, Ray, to check?' I forgot to explain how his legs might be measured, assuming that an Anglican priest would know all about it, so I was bemused to see him eagerly take off his shoes and lie full length on the carpet.

'Right,' he said cheerfully, 'I'm ready.'

He looked a little like a giant toy soldier, arms laid stiffly by his sides and waiting for major surgery: the sight of this priest laid full-length on the floor of this room did not help my composure. I recalled that the next step was to look at his ankle bones. Nothing seemed drastically wrong as I had seen with Sandra; just an eighth-of-an-inch of misalignment. We prayed as a group — how glad I was that this was the prayer, not of an individual, but a body of people. I looked at the legs again and it seemed as if they were the same length, but it was not possible to be decisive.

Ray later told us his story. He had had a most painful back condition for years as a result of the short leg, even though he had worn a lifter in the appropriate shoe. He was regularly examined and treated by a specialist who, as a matter of course, began every examination by measuring his legs. Ray was due for a further examination the next week, but its normal course was interrupted by the specialist losing his temper with his secretary as he accused her of giving him the wrong file: the recorded leg measurements on the file did not match those of the patient before him. The patient, exclaimed the specialist, had two legs the same length whereas the record of the file was of odd-length legs.

That was the sort of evidence that appealed to me, yet I had to learn that it was not upon that evidence that faith was based: the evidence was merely the justification of the faith and consequential upon it. How different was this approach to all of that in my training. As an engineer I had been taught that seeing was believing, a phrase used widely in the world. Principles stated in the lecture-room were demonstrated in the laboratory and then I was expected to embrace them: my understanding worked upon the evidence at the test bench, to combine what I saw with compact statements at the lecture desk. As a Christian I was to learn that the opposite was true: the principle upon which I believed resulted in the demonstration.

A cynical world, of which I had always been part, was saying, 'I will see in order that I might believe,' but the Lord God was saying to me, 'You will believe in order that you might see.' The manifestation of the outworking of the original principle would be no less tangible because of the Lord's preferred order of events: for example, the growth of Ray's leg was accurately measured in the best medical way. There was, though, an order set that brought all men to the same common level, where their natural personal attributes counted for nothing, giving no one an advantage over another: the only attribute used was the God-given one of faith: 'Through faith, we understand . . .'

★   ★   ★

Chairs always presented a problem at the meetings: often there were not enough of them, so people sat on the floor as necessary. We obtained a variety of stacking chairs ranging from relatively comfortable tubular-steel to very uncomfortable wooden devices, designed I felt, by the man who invented the mousetrap but who, in this instance, had human fingers in mind.

New faces were often seen at the meetings and one evening a lady, who was a stranger to us, was sat on one of the mousetrap chairs next to Elizabeth. As the evening progressed, so did her fidgeting.

At the conclusion of the meeting people exchanged social chit-chat and she engaged in conversation with Elizabeth sharing, eventually, in the greatest confidence, 'If I ever come to this place again I'll be sure to get a more comfortable seat. I don't know what sort of people the owners of this house could be, to put out chairs like this for us to sit upon.'

Elizabeth nodded sagely and then half an hour or so later we saw the lady's discomfort growing as, red-faced, she realized that since Elizabeth was the only person remaining in the room, she was one of the 'owners of this house.'

Her comment was however nothing to that of a visitor who, looking around the hallway of our house, asked me in innocence and horror at what he saw, 'Do people actually live in this place?'

Such observations were transcended by a conversation one Saturday morning with a total stranger in the main street of Ampthill. It was a Red Cross flag day and she

was selling the little flags that are worn in the button-
hole.

Buying one, I saw my opportunity to do my evangelistic
good turn for the day, so looking intently at the flag in
my hand I asked, 'Do you know what the cross means?'

'It's the symbol of our organization,' she replied.

'Yes, but does the cross mean anything else?' I pursued.

'I don't think so.'

'Well, it's also the symbol of the Christian, for it brings
to mind the fact that Jesus died for us.'

Looking a little guilty at being caught out she answered,
'Oh, of course. I used to be a Sunday School teacher you
know.'

Then continuing, she added, 'I know some other
people who talk like you: they live in Church Avenue.'
This was next to our own street, Church Street. 'In fact
they have Christian meetings in their home.' I was now
thoroughly alerted. If there were meetings so close, why
hadn't I heard about them? I asked for more details.
'Oh, wonderful meetings, we have.' She was warming to
her subject and was evidently a central figure in the whole
thing. Details poured out of the most amazing events,
but I was assured that it was all nicely done — the couple
in whose house the meetings took place were both school-
teachers, I was told, so that made everything all right.
Reaching the climax of her story, she exhorted me to go
there sometime to find out all about it and I said that I
would love to — could she give me the address?

'I don't recall the exact number,' she said, 'but we
meet upstairs in a place called the Upper Room.'

I looked at her in blank amazement as I recalled that
Ray's wife had once referred to our drawing room on
the first-floor of the house, where our meetings were
held, as the Upper Room, a name which had stuck with
one or two people. This total stranger was inviting me to
go to my own home to attend a meeting which I regularly
led! I couldn't bring myself to deflate her enthusiasm so,
lamely assured her that I would be there at the first
available opportunity and fled, flag in hand. For weeks I
anxiously viewed the people coming to the meeting in

case she was there: a confrontation would have been most embarrassing. As it happens I never saw her again, nor could I recall ever having seen her at any previous meeting.

★ ★ ★

The Ampthill Fellowship, as the regular Thursday meetings came to be known, passed through a zenith and then went into a period of decline. We couldn't understand why this should be, for there was a large measure of unity there and a sincere desire to honour the Lord. For myself, I had a difficulty with one regular visitor: this I wrote off as a personality problem. Yet with the advance of time I came to recognize that a glance at this Christian's face, upon arrival at a meeting, was enough to tell me if we were going to have a profitable or a dry evening.

The numbers continued to decline and one evening, in response to a question from a speaker who was soon to be with us, I mentioned obliquely that we had one or two problems.

After ministering at the meeting a day later, he drew me to one side, pointed out my friend with whom I had the personality difficulty and said, 'That is the centre of your problem. That person has the spirit of divination.'

I didn't know what he was talking about, yet exactly the same message was repeated by a further visiting speaker the next week. A few days later I had to fly to the USA on business and, because of a mistake in arrangements, found myself stuck in Dulles Airport, Washington DC for several hours. Idling my time away I phoned a friend in Georgia and during the conversation he asked me how things were going in the Ampthill Fellowship. I tried to be truthful, mentioning in passing the apparent personality problem.

'Hey, that's the spirit of divination,' he explained.

Within days I was in Toronto, Canada where I was met by Merv, who had sung at our open-air concert, and we shared a little following their earlier visit to the area.

'How are things going there?' he asked. Cautiously I
reported the situation, careful not to put in anything
that might indicate the way that people had in the past
week or two been speaking to me.

'Hold on,' he exclaimed, 'I know this problem. That's
the spirit of divination.'

Recognizing the scriptural injunction that it is in the
mouths of two or three witnesses that matters are established, I decided to do something. Firstly I read the appropriate verses in Acts 16 to find out what the spirit of
divination was, then looked up in the Bible the correct
way to deal with a problem. Remembering to approach
the whole matter in a spirit of love rather than antagon-
ism, there was an attempt to minister to the problem,
but the advances were rejected and the subject of the
'personality problem' left us. It was a saddening moment
for there had, in spite of the difficulty, been much by
way of fellowship over the years and I think that I may
have begun to feel something of the concern that a pastor has when people leave a fellowship in other than
good standing.

This was certainly the bleakest moment in the life of
the fellowship: the damage, it seemed, had been done
and nearly everyone had given up attending. It was one
of those moments when we put it to the Lord that we
should close the meetings. The next Thursday as I
prayed, the Lord gave me a word to share in the evening, but by the beginning of the meeting there was just
one person present. I decided that since I had a word
from God, it was to be ministered, so prepared to launch
it upon that one man. As it happened, two more people
arrived late, with Elizabeth and me making the total of
five: it was a good evening.

From that moment we saw the Lord build the meeting
again, from what we were to recognize as a new start. If
there was one distinctively different feature in the meetings now, it was that the Lord impressed upon us a need
for continuity in the ministry of the word. Hitherto, while
we had always looked for some teaching at every meeting, we had always believed that God would burden

somebody's heart to teach something. The Lord had always honoured that declaration of faith but it had not resulted in the growth that might have been expected. As the numbers again grew I found myself interested in searching the scripture on the subject of 'priesthood'. Eventually I felt that I had enough data to fill one, or perhaps, two evenings of teaching and was more than surprised when the series lasted for six weeks. It was at that point I felt someone else should take over. I was aware that the Lord was speaking to my heart on 'Faith' and Hebrews 11 had taken on a very lively appearance, but I was determined that I had done enough by way of teaching.

The following Thursday evening we gathered, prayed, sang and waited. Nothing happened, no one shared a scripture, yet within me there was a convicting voice calling me to teach on 'Faith'. I held my ground, determined not to be moved — perhaps I didn't have the faith to be obedient to the Lord.

Finally, Terry, who was considering resigning his profession to go to theological college spoke, 'I know that it's not the done thing to share this in Christian company, but there are many times when I do not have faith.' He went on to voice the difficulty, common among Christians and, we realized, common within the group of people present, of being called to lead a life of faith and yet, at times, failing miserably. 'What is to be done?' he concluded.

Conviction weighed heavily upon me and I knew that every moment of silence on my part was a moment of disobedience before the Lord.

Finally I said, 'Let's take a look at Hebrews, chapter 11 and verse 1.' The series lasted more than a year.

It was the centrality of our examination of the Bible that brought any maturity to the Fellowship. The miracles continued as prayer was answered, Christian ladies saw their husbands converted and the sick were healed, but one feature brought more rejoicing than anything else. It wasn't a leg that we all saw grow over four inches; neither was it the astonishing incident of a man who was

on his way to London Airport to return to an illicit relationship with a woman abroad, but suddenly found
himself compelled to come to the meeting to repent as
we were praying for him. No, it was something we saw
happening over a period of time. In the last three to
four years that the meeting ran I cannot recall one unconverted person who came to the meeting, who left
without becoming a Christian. It wasn't that, upon entry,
we hit them with a box full of evangelistic verses: they
found the presence of the Lord Jesus to be real enough
to convince and convict them.

13

Children in Crisis

Our first two children, Matthew and Rachel, were born before we had become Christians so that, small as they were at the time, they saw the changes in our lives as they lived in our own home. Naturally we were, for our part, keen to know of the spiritual position of our own children: certainly it was a thought, consistent with our own discovery, that they too needed to be born again; but when? Could a small child be a Christian? After all, we couldn't expect a very young person to understand the doctrines surrounding conversion, nor could we expect a child to change a lifestyle just because the Bible said so. It's surprising how quickly we had forgotten the circumstances around our own conversions, building instead a scenario that would like to demand a short course at Bible School as a minimum requirement for becoming a Christian. I realize that I had not understood the doctrines surrounding conversion when I had been born again: I hadn't even been aware of the place of Calvary in the scheme of things. Further, the life-changing effects had come about before I knew one end of my Bible from the other. That being the case, I was brought to the conclusion that my entry to the Christian life was motivated by the grace of God and realized through the exercise of faith. It was self-evident that the grace was entirely of God and by God and even the faith had been given by him. In that circumstance, my personal qualifications, whether of age or intellect, had not been contributory and if they carried no weight in my case, it must follow that they carried no weight for my children. I could then see no reason why a small child should not be a Christian in just as full a sense as I was.

Elizabeth and I prayed for them both and, with the later arrival of David, prayed for him also: in one form or another, those prayers have continued over the years. The Bible, we later learned, had many good things to say about the parent/child relationship, but at this stage in our lives, it was their salvation in particular for which we prayed.

Matthew had just passed his fourth birthday when, one day, he asked his mother, 'Mummy, am I a Christian?'

'No, you aren't,' Elizabeth responded.

'Why is that?' came the further question. Elizabeth explained what a Christian is and how a person becomes one.

'That's what I want,' Matthew replied firmly, and, so saying, he sat on his mother's knee, asked the Lord to forgive him the sin of his life and gave himself to God. It could have been a theologically correct set of words uttered in obedience to a routine, but it wasn't. A young child had sought the Lord with all his heart and there is no doubt that simple observation of his subsequent life brought the evidence that his seeking had had its reward — he was born again.

Rachel was, in her turn, four years old, when she met me on my return home from the office one evening, with the statement, 'Daddy, I've asked Jesus into my heart — because I wanted to.'

She was the singer in the family: often we would hear her singing in bed in the mornings and again when she was being prepared for bed in the evening. Three years after her conversion we were on holiday in Scotland when, one evening, as Elizabeth was getting her to bed, she began to sing. Suddenly she stopped and looked at her mother in surprise and the look was returned as both mother and daughter realized that the singing was not in English, or any tongue that they had ever heard. The perfectly formed melodic language of those moments was the evidence to a little girl that she had just been baptized in the Holy Spirit in accordance with the scriptures.

★   ★   ★

The winter weather had suddenly worsened with heavy snow in Scotland and North Wales. Roads had been closed by drifting snow in several places and in particular, the main road through the Welsh mountains to Colwyn Bay, where I had a weekend of speaking engagements, was impassable. It was Friday evening and I was vexed at the thought of missing the Saturday meetings. Instead of being on the road north, I was sat at home: Elizabeth and I were reading while David, at three-and-a-half years of age, was playing with toys on the floor.

The silence, which was punctuated only by the occasional rustle of the newspaper and the movement of David's toys on the carpet, was broken by Elizabeth speaking in a low, yet concerned voice. 'Roy, do you notice anything strange about David?'

'What do you mean?'

'Just look at his eyes: I think that there's something wrong with them.'

Glancing at the child, I spoke quite sharply to Elizabeth. 'Nonsense, there's nothing wrong with his eyes. What are you trying to say?'

'Well, once or twice in the last couple of weeks I've noticed that they don't always appear to be completely straight and I saw it again, just now.' The concern in her voice was now quite evident and became more heightened as we watched David closely. He was reaching out in the general direction of a toy and then grasping at air about twelve inches to one side of it.

Eventually he looked up, saying, 'Mummy, why is it that when I reach out for one of my toys, it won't come into my hand?'

His look in our direction was enough to confirm Elizabeth's fears: David was going cross-eyed. We watched in horror as, over the next couple of hours, the misalignment became progressively more pronounced until the eyes were twenty-five degrees out of line, as a later examination revealed.

By the time that we went to bed, David had two desperately worried parents as well as the confusion, to his small life, of serious double vision. We did all the things that good Christian parents might do. We prayed for him and we took him to the doctor. The problem was outside of the domain of a general practitioner, so David was immediately referred to specialists. An examination provided no good cheer: there was no apparent reason why the problem had occurred but our real worry lay in what we were told for the future. Both eyes were still functioning correctly, we learned, but the brain would discriminate between the two images presented, progressively selecting one. The other eye would suffer an irreversible condition of blindness which would be complete in about a year. Surgery was the only solution offered and how long would it be before the surgery could be done?

'The waiting list is eighteen months.' We were stunned as we heard the words. Could anything be done? After advice we found that it would be possible to arrange an operation within the next three to four months, but we were also warned that every week we waited would result in a deterioration of the eyes that could not be countered. Further, we learned that the operation was not always successful.

Our praying for David continued: of course the Lord could heal him, his word said so and our experience over several years as we had seen others receiving such a touch from God confirmed that word. We didn't know how it might be done: perhaps by a miracle, perhaps even through surgery. We wanted the former.

The time for the surgery approached and, with it, the intensity of our prayers for David's eyes increased. The conviction that the Lord might miraculously straighten the eyes never left us. In fact the reports we were getting from the ophthalmologist encouraged us in the knowledge that the Lord had his hand upon the whole matter: each eye was maintaining its own eyesight undiminished against the predictions that had been made. It was described to us on one occasion that David's brain was continually switching from the signal of one eye to that of the other, neither eye being preferred. From the fact that this was mentioned to us, it was clearly regarded by the specialists as being very unusual.

Nevertheless the time arrived to go to the hospital about twenty miles away. I drove Elizabeth and David there, leaving Elizabeth to spend the night before the operation in the small ward with him. I was back again early in the morning and sat with Elizabeth as he was prepared for the short trip to the operating theatre. Our hearts could hardly have been heavier than that moment when we watched him, dressed in a white gown and looking a little frightened, being wheeled out of the ward and down the corridor.

We wept and prayed, knowing that our God would not forsake us. Perhaps the miracle would occur on the operating table: even as the surgeon's knife was in his hand he might see David's eyes straightening — what a witness that would be to the Lord.

It was about three hours later that we learned that that had happened. David, still under the anaesthetic, was wheeled back to his ward, his eyes heavily bandaged. As Elizabeth prepared to spend the next couple of nights with him, we felt confused, but, glad that the operation was complete, waited to see the bandages taken off. She was given strict instructions regarding what she could do: David was to have no liquid until the following day when the effects of the anaesthetic would be worn off and the chances of vomiting eliminated.

It was a bad night. David had woken and was desperate for water: he was evidently in considerable pain. Beyond praying for him and consoling him there was nothing that his mother could do. As she prayed, there came clearly to her mind, 'Cast your burden upon the Lord . . . and he will sustain you,' a quotation from Psalm 55 (verse 22, Amplified Bible). In the midst of that troublesome moment, a great peace overwhelmed her and then she heard David say, 'It's all right, Mummy:

the pain has gone now.'

It had and he never had any further pain, a feature
that runs counter to the post-operational experience of
those who have such surgery. For Elizabeth, there was a
further beautiful touch in evidence of the Lord's word
and his working. Several days later she returned home,
and tearing the backlog of sheets from the daily calen-
dar, she noticed that, for the date of David's operation,
March 21st, there was printed the quotation, 'Cast your
burden upon the Lord and he will sustain you,' — the
same verse as she had received!

Three days later the bandages came off and we were
able to see the result. There was an improvement but it
had to be admitted that the operation could not be described as a success: there was still a misalignment of ten
degrees or so. Our confusion increased and became the
greater when a week or so later, we learned that scar-
tissue was now forming on the eye that had been the
subject of the surgery.

'It can be dealt with,' we were told, 'it will need a
further, but minor, operation to get rid of it.' A further
operation! We couldn't stand the thought as we recalled
the agony of the last few weeks and we cried out to God
again. By now we hardly knew how to pray, but we were
desperate.

There was another appointment for David three
weeks after the operation and the eye was closely
scrutinized.

After a lengthy examination, the specialist said, 'This
is most strange: I can't find the scar-tissue. It seems to
have disappeared, but scar-tissue doesn't disappear.' In
spite of the heartaches we had been through when
everything seemed black and there was so little evidence
that prayer was being met, our hearts rejoiced as we
knew this to be a welcome sign that the Lord God was
still active in David's problems.

It must have been about eighteen months after the
eye problem had begun that, one afternoon, I was chair-
ing a meeting of my research team in the office when
the telephone on my desk rang. It was Elizabeth, and I

could detect anxiety in her voice.

'Roy, could you come home at once.'

'Of course I can't come home, Elizabeth: I'm in the middle of a meeting.'

'But Roy, please come — it's David.' Elizabeth began to weep as she told me that he had collapsed and she had thought he had died.

All thought of scientific research, contract dates, funds and manpower vanished from my mind.

'Call the doctor to the house at once — I'm coming right away.' I tried to sound calm as I put the telephone down, dismissed the meeting and then hurried to my car.

It was well that I knew the country road to my home and there was never much traffic upon it. Every corner took rubber from the tyres while the car was driven as never before and the ten miles was covered in about as many minutes.

Before the doctor had got across the village I arrived at my house and rushed in. Elizabeth was in David's bedroom in tears and there on the bed was David. I had never seen a dead child and had no idea of what I was looking at. I couldn't form a judgement but I could see that the face, which always had the English characteristics of rosy cheeks, was a uniform grey colour, and the region around the eyes was black.

There are moments in life when one learns what prayer is all about: it cannot be taught in a classroom and it can't be learned from a book. Our prayer lives grow from those first self-centred intonations of a young Christian to the contemplative intercessions of the saint who sits before the Lord waiting to know from God how to pray in a particular situation. But suddenly, our ordered way of doing things is shattered by the un-expected, and prayer is also subject to such unplanned events. Nehemiah found this as he prayed for Jerusalem, having heard the bad news about it. Elijah found it also as he prayed for the dead son of the widow of Zarephath. For Elijah, it wasn't a case of wondering if this was his type of prayer or even seeking to know the will of God in the matter: he prayed.

Standing at David's bed, so did we. I learned what prayer was as I cried out to God for my son's life: then after a few minutes the doctor arrived. As we heard his footsteps on the staircase I noticed, in David's face, that a pink colour was beginning to displace the grey of the cheeks and I knew that the body before me had circulation.

During the doctor's examination, David, to our great relief, regained consciousness, but our joy became somewhat muted as we were given a grave prognosis. The problem had nothing to do with the eye condition but, again, this was a matter for specialists. The result of the examination was that an ongoing series of drugs was prescribed which, we were told, he would probably need to take for the rest of his life. At birth, David had been very healthy, as well as the heaviest of our children. His good health had been maintained through the first three-and-a-half years of his life so that until his eye problem had called for the doctor's attention, there wasn't even a medical card in existence for David at the surgery. After those trouble-free years we now had a son who we knew to have impaired eyesight. We were told he needed drugs on a continuing basis and a result of the drugs was a change of personality into a rather temperamental child. We didn't know why this happened or what we should do about it.

It was some months later that Elizabeth commented to me. 'Do you remember that vision Gladys told me about before David was born?' I didn't recall who Gladys was, much less her vision. I was reminded that she was a lady who had lived in the next village and with whom Elizabeth had occasional fellowship before Gladys had moved abroad.

'She visited me one day shortly before David was born to say that, during that morning while praying, she had seen a vision in which I was pushing a perambulator along a street. On the side of the perambulator there was a large poster carrying the words "A Testimony to the Lord's Healing."'

'She said what?' My interest was strangely quickened and, as the story of five to six years before was repeated, I knew that we had the word for which we had been seeking the Lord.

In jubilation I said, 'That's it — that's the word of God for us — David will be a testimony to the healing of the Lord!' Our prayer-life for David was galvanized from that moment: no longer were we beaten, pleading for the Lord to do something. We knew what his intention was and we could now pray with confidence to that end. We didn't know how long it would be, but we did know that David was going to be healed.

Some months later I had to go to Toronto to interview a candidate for my research team. It was a busy period and after one night in Canada I had a business appointment in Indiana, USA. Again I was planning just one night in Indianapolis where I was grateful for close friends at whose home I could stay, relieving the monotony of hotels. Chuck met me at the airport and I had dinner with him, his wife and another guest on the veranda of his home.

It was a perfect spring evening and after dinner, I was beginning to relax as I relished the first evening without engagements for about six weeks, when Chuck commented to me, 'There's a meeting this evening.' Knowing my friend, I realized that it was a Christian meeting to which he referred. I didn't want to give up this free time but realizing that it would be impolite not to fit in with any arrangements, I responded,

'Oh good. Who is the speaker?'

'You are,' was the short and chilling answer. I looked at Chuck with ill-concealed horror.

'What time does the meeting begin?' I asked, fearing the worst and I got it.

'At eight o'clock.' It was three minutes to eight o'clock.

In moments we were seated in the meeting, my mind in a whirl. At least, I knew that there would be a time of singing, sharing, praying — all the things that Christians do, while I would think of something to say.

'We're going to begin with a short prayer,' announced

Chuck, 'and then I'm going to ask Roy to speak.' And short it was! My prayer was also short — and desperate: I needed a word from the Lord. I was still fumbling for my Bible as I rose and knew the Lord speaking a word into my heart — Mark 4:35. Reading the story of the stilling of the storm on the Sea of Galilee, I shared two points.

Jesus had said, 'Let us pass over unto the other side,' and they had his word. From the moment that Jesus gave the word, there was to be no question about it — they were going to the other side. He had said nothing about what they would go through to get there — there could be all sorts of difficulties in the way and indeed they were to find that this would be so, but of one thing they could be certain: they were going to the other side. Such was the essence of faith: by the Lord, a word given to which they could hold through all the vicissitudes of the journey, as it defined the will of God for that moment and specified their destiny. These men were going to get to the other side.

When the storm blew up, he was with them in the boat. What a comfort this should have been to this group of fishermen. They had tried everything that their professional training had to offer, but they were in difficulties for they were still shipping water. In the crisis they need only to have recognized the presence of their divine passenger — he would always be with them, even unto the end of the age — and there should have been the re-assuring calm in their beings, a knowledge that his presence was as reliable as his word.

I explained the beauty of this pattern as it applies to Christian lives today: the presence of the Lord is to bring peace into the storm of our lives for he's there in every storm and his word always holds true — we're going to get to the other side.

It was as I was concluding my comments that I knew the Lord to be prompting me to tell the story of David. This I did, and when I related Gladys's vision, I said, 'Just as the disciples had the word of the Lord we have the word of the Lord for David.'

Emotion rose within as the realization broke upon me that the Lord was taking me along the particular path of which I had that evening been speaking and which led to one conclusion.

I continued, 'This night I declare to you, my David is healed.' It was nine o'clock in the evening.

I might not have spoken with such assurance had I known that, back in England, David was very ill. His temperature had escalated, a danger-sign in the drug-related problem. Elizabeth's concern was at a high level as she sat by his bedside all day, praying for him. She had, during that prayer, asked the Lord to give her a word.

'Let us pass over unto the other side,' the word of the Lord came to her.

She asked the Lord for a further word.

'I'm in the midst of the storm,' came the answer. We had never discussed that scripture in Mark's gospel and Elizabeth certainly had no idea that I was speaking on this or any other subject at that time, but, incredibly, the same word was being ministered by the Holy Spirit to her as to me and through me, four-and-a-half-thousand miles away.

At three o'clock in the morning a miracle occurred in David's bedroom as, suddenly, his temperature reverted to normal. From that moment he no longer needed to take the prescribed drugs and from that time we began to see his eyes straightening.

Nine o'clock in the evening in Indianapolis when I made that declaration was three o'clock in the morning in England when the Lord brought his healing touch.

That was not the end of the matter, though, and several times there was the temptation to re-introduce the drugs. This was no light matter for we knew that the future of our son's health and, as a result, his whole life-style, depended upon us walking in obedience to the Lord. Of course, every time that there seemed to be reason for administering the drugs there was the question: 'Was it the Lord who we had heard previously, or was it a fabrication of our minds?' Whenever this point arose, we had to check through everything that had happened and then, convinced of the word we had received from the Lord, we were obedient to it.

While the drug-related problem was thus dealt with, we continued in our praying for David's eyes. The regular examinations continued, sometimes with encouraging results, but sometimes we were discouraged by what we heard.

After one particular series of tests using pictures on cards we were told, 'David does not have three-dimensional vision and he never will have.'

On another occasion we were warned that while there was a substantial improvement in the alignment of his eyes, they would probably go wrong again when he began serious study at school. At one particularly dark moment, further surgery was suggested to effect a straightening. But we had the word of God and we continued to pray. For his part, David wore spectacles and accordingly suffered at school from being different to the other children in having to use them.

As time advanced the progressive reduction in the misalignment could be clearly seen and, in consequence, he was prescribed appropriately weaker lenses in his spectacles. By now the examinations were taking place at six-monthly intervals but this pattern was disturbed by a family move to the USA for a year. It was then fourteen months later that David had his next appointment for which we had prayed much, looking to the Lord to fulfil his promise as David would be told that he would not need to wear spectacles again.

From the specialist's point of view the inspection was a success: there had been no deterioration over that period and he ordered the lens prescription for David to remain unchanged. For us it was a grave disappointment: there had been no improvement.

I returned immediately to the USA and Elizabeth spent four days seeking the Lord in the matter. As he spoke to her she felt that she must pray for David with the laying-on of hands. This was no great novelty to David for he had seen such prayer from time to time in the home.

It was a couple of days later that David, returning from school, had his spelling-book with him for some homework. Elizabeth, trained as a schoolteacher, always watched his progress but, glancing through the spelling-book on this day, noticed several mistakes in the most recent entries.

'David,' she admonished, 'where did you get these spellings from?'

'I copied them from the blackboard,' he replied.

'Now you couldn't have done so, because your teacher wouldn't put incorrect spellings on the board. You must be more careful in the future and check the spellings on the board.' The schoolteacher in Elizabeth was emerging.

'But Mummy,' said David, slightly pained, 'I can't see what it says on the blackboard. It's all fuzzy.'

Elizabeth was thoroughly alarmed and cross-questioned him. He hadn't moved his location in the class and, it transpired that the blackboard wasn't 'fuzzy' all the time.

'When I look at the blackboard like this,' he volunteered peering normally through his spectacles, 'it's all fuzzy, but when I look like this,' he added, perching his spectacles on the end of his nose and looking over them, 'I can see perfectly.'

'I'm taking you back to the eye-specialist,' said his alarmed mother.

'But Mummy,' was David's last comment, 'don't you remember that you prayed for me two days ago? Perhaps Jesus has healed me.'

We returned to the specialist and he was clearly triumphant at the turn of events.

'There is a marked improvement,' I was told, but because I'm a very conservative man, I'm going to prescribe lenses for him. The new prescription for one eye is virtually plain glass though and the other lens isn't much different.' It was about this time that the same set of test cards was again produced to examine three-dimensionality in his vision and we learned that David

now had three-dimensional vision. We knew that the
Lord, having given his word, was keeping it and the
growing series of medical reports was charting the progress in the hand of God.

It was just a year later that David had his next examination. Again the results were good, but reviewing
all the reports at his disposal, the specialist finally concluded that David would, nevertheless, wear spectacles
for the rest of his life. We felt heart-broken for our son
who walked away in tears, but the Lord had brought
him so far that it seemed inconceivable the work would
not be completed.

Just a few days later we had an unexpected telephone
call from the ophthalmologist. Could they have another
look at David and could it be before Christmas, because
it was just possible that they might have some news that
would be a Christmas present for him? It was with un-
alloyed joy that we learned, following this examination,
that David need no longer wear spectacles!

But there was more to come. After a subsequent examination six months later we were told that David now
had normal three-dimensional vision: we had not been
informed that, at earlier examinations, his had been an
abnormal three-dimensional vision. 'When the abnormal type is established,' we were told, 'it's most unusual
for the normal vision to return.' Further, the report was
that David now had eyesight better than that expected
for a child of his age.

It had been a long road. The word of the Lord had
come eleven years earlier, before David was born. It was
about eighteen months after the second illness had over-
taken him that we had known that moment when we
could claim God's word to be manifested. It had been
seven years from seeing him groping for his toys on the
carpet to having the report confirming the fullness of
healing of David's eyes. We had learned a little over
those years. Our respect for the medical people who
cared for him could not have been higher and their
dedication and skill was beyond any praise that we could
give. We had also learned a little of waiting on the Lord

and we had discovered that, by the same word, he had brought instantaneous and complete healing of one problem, but a gradual healing of another. Further, in his plan, the Lord God had used medical specialists and not ignored abilities that he had invested in them. There was a body of carefully measured evidence, fully documented, that would always bear testimony to the events through which we had lived. For me, as a scientist, that had its own satisfaction, even if there had been a price to pay to get to this point. Yet there was a higher level of satisfaction than that: our son, for whom it seemed there was to be a life of partial blindness and a personality affected by prescribed drugs, was whole. In the wholeness that was now his, we clearly saw the intervening and loving hand of God, fulfilling his promises, his way.

Can a child's conversion and Christian walk be as valid as that of an adult? One by one we had watched our children give their lives to the Lord, not as a result of parental pressure, but because they wanted to. In fact, because of our fear that they could, in attempting to emulate their parents, have made a false start which would have been damaging later on, we had rather discouraged any commitment from such young children. Because of the individual commitments they had made, though, there emerged lives that had an awareness of the Lord God and there can be no doubt that theirs were the lives of regenerate people. By that new birth they had had, they became the beneficiaries of all that the Lord has for his people.

Many years later, Matthew was living in London reading for a law degree. His bedroom needed a re-organization so, resignedly, Elizabeth faced up to the job, as any mother who has to make an occasional expedition into the hinterland of a son's bedroom. As she was moving books she came across a small notebook. Opening it, she found inside a series of entries, badly spelt and written in a rather untidy hand. The headline of the front page read, 'How Jesus has spoken to me.' Beneath, was an entry which, with corrected spelling, read:

A little later in that year I woke up about midnight and went to my bedroom door and opened it. Our front staircase is very winding and is opposite my room and looks like this. (A drawing of the staircase with draughtsmanship of a standard similar to the spelling, was inserted here.) As I was looking at the staircase — it was a pitch black night — I saw a very bright light on the roof above the staircase. It got closer: I was not frightened. Then he stood next to the banisters which are opposite my room. He did not say a thing to me: he looked at me with his loving eyes. I just felt he loved me: when I saw him I just loved him so much. He wore a long white garment: not man's sort of white, but a white like clean snow. He did not wear anything on his feet. He had a very close gingery beard, but it was not ginger: it was a pale brown and orange. His face was loving. On his head, instead of a crown of thorns, he had a crown of glory: it was just a white light but, boy, it was white — it dazzled me. It was lighter than snow: it was silver-white. I'm afraid I cannot describe his face because I was most of the time looking at his feet as I realized I nailed him to the cross. All I can say about it was that it was so loving. Then as silently as he had come, he walked into the spare bedroom singing, 'This is my story, this is my song, praising my Saviour all the day long,' and whistling parts of it as I got back to bed I heard God say to me, 'You are my son in whom I am well pleased.'

8 years 11 months old

14
Which Way?

The battle had commenced in a Huntingdonshire village and reached significant proportions at the desk in my office in the engineering laboratory at Cambridge. I had no idea where the outcome would take me and still often wonder where it is my family and I are aimed at. It is clear that as the disciples followed Jesus they didn't know where he was taking them, so there has been the consolation of finding myself in good company. Yet the uncertainty of the path with all its intermediate destinations, even if the final destination is well defined, encourages the doubts that assail the mind. In this I've been no exception and perhaps, because of the structured style of my scientific training and the well-defined aims in all my engineering work, this has been — and continues to be — an even greater problem.

The first exposure in a church pulpit in Exmoor had led to circuit preaching in Methodist churches in Derbyshire and Staffordshire. That brought frightening, exciting and often hilarious moments: frightening as one faced congregations formidable in looks if not in size, exciting as week by week one saw people respond to the word shared and hilarious as church organ keys jammed, emitting uncontrolled high-pitch squeaks, or as the preacher's seat tipped up under his weight. Much of what happened may not have been theologically deepening but it produced experience that could never be forgotten. It was disquieting to see a congregation flee through the door at the end of the service to avoid having to shake

hands with the preacher after his convicting address —
and what is more to be in such a rush that two people
actually got jammed in the doorway. (It should be recorded in fairness that it was rather a narrow door and they
were quite fat people!) Yet it was a pleasure to hear, from
time to time someone say, after a service, 'I've been praying for years that the Lord would send us that word.'

As we moved southwards from Derby, further avenues
of Christian expression began to open in England. This
coincided with a career challenge and opportunity that
was more than I could ever have hoped for in the wildest
excursions of my imagination as a shop-boy in an engineering workshop: the invitation to build a research laboratory from scratch. It indeed took many years to produce
the structure, whose plan developed progressively in my
mind, but over that time a strong team of men gathered
around the work.

It was thus into a well-ordered life, albeit with some
clash of interest between the time devoted to Christian
work and that devoted to secular work, that a small pebble
was dropped one day. As in a pond, the ripples didn't die
but grew in influence to unforeseen dimensions. I was, at
that time, a member of the Gideons, whose excellent work
in placing Bibles in the traffic lanes of life, is well known.
One of the activities of the Gideons, known as church
assignments, involved me in visiting a church locally to
share the Gideon story. It was at the end of the meeting
that, talking to the pastor on an entirely unrelated matter,
he said, 'Perhaps the Lord will use you to minister for him
as you travel in connection with your work.' It was an odd
statement, since, beyond a short visit to Brussels, I had
never travelled in connection with my work: yet it was
startling since I knew that the Holy Spirit was anointing it
to my ears and hammering it into my heart. I responded,
'I receive that from the Lord.'

The pastor looked startled and, to correct any misunder-
standing said, 'Now please don't do anything about it. I
must say that I felt no anointing when I made the comment
and wouldn't want you to presume that it was a word from
the Lord.'

'Isn't it marvellous,' I replied, 'that the Lord can use us and we don't even know it?'

At least I had the strong feeling that here was direction from the Lord God — I was going to travel — and in connection with my work. Things began to move quickly and in twenty-four hours I was, by request, in the US Embassy in London discussing an invitation from the US government to do a lecture tour of research facilities in the USA on a 'Window on Science' programme. Immediately I also had a separate call to a scientific conference in Canada to deliver two research papers. The prospect became more exciting as a passport was obtained, a suitcase of Victorian design and manufacture was exhumed from the attic, and papers and clothes were prepared.

There was just one thing that made the preparation less than joyful: Elizabeth was facing, with evident difficulty, the thought of our separation for a period of time. Much of our early married life had included times of separation, college work and job changes all taking their toll, but at least I had always been in the same country and hence, easily contactable. This was going to be different and the fears of this particular unknown were having their effects.

It was some years before that we had first met Jean, as she began an itinerant ministry in England.

Praying with Elizabeth one day, she had said, 'Elizabeth, I see a hair-line crack running right from the foundation of your life, which the Lord will fill up with himself.'

What this crack could be, we didn't know. Matters finally came to a head when a group from the Ampthill Fellowship were praying for me in connection with that first journey abroad. Elizabeth felt a great separation from me and went to her room. It was there that the Lord ministered to her, taking her back to the time that she was a small child. Her mother had died when she was a little over a year old and she saw the insecurity that had resulted in her life.

As she became aware of this, the Lord spoke to her, 'It's perfectly all right: there's nothing to be afraid of.'

There was an immediate peace and the torment of years passed away. The relief was not entire in that moment, but was progressive as she rested upon the word that the Lord God had given her. The Lord had shown to her, and dealt with, the crack running from the foundation of her life. This was not the work of amateur psychiatrists using spiritual phraseology and claiming to have a special ministry, prying into people's backgrounds: it was a sovereign work of God, executed in his time, his way.

It was as well that this was placed before the Master right at the beginning of my travelling because the times of separation we were to have became far greater than we would have ever expected: in some ways we see this as the greatest price we have ever had to choose to pay to obey the will of God.

The first transatlantic trip was full of the adventure of new experiences, and it happens that there is still an excited schoolboy jumping up and down inside of me on every aeroplane flight. The scientific aspects of the itinerary went well but, surprisingly, in free periods I kept meeting Christians, stumbling on churches or having the most remarkable opportunities to talk to people of the faith I had found in Jesus Christ. During that time, while speaking at one church, to my astonishment, I saw the congregation of about 150 rise to its feet, weeping in repentance before the Lord.

In the 'Window on Science' lecture tour I was a guest of the US government and was treated accordingly. At every location I was hosted by a senior officer of the United States Air Force and every need was attended to. It was thus in Ohio that I met Gerry, my host and guide for a few days.

In our first conversation he invited me to take dinner at his home, commenting that I must by then be fed up with hotel and restaurant food. I was glad at the prospect of entering a family atmosphere for the first time in a couple of weeks, and the next evening I was taken to his house. The dinner was almost ready when we arrived and Gerry's wife asked me what I would care to drink with my meal. I had already learned that coffee was apparently regarded as more vital than oxygen to most people I had met during the tour, so said that I would have coffee.

'We don't drink coffee, but I'll make some for you,' responded my hostess.

'In that case, I'll be happy to have tea,' I countered.

'We don't drink tea either,' I heard her say. Alarm bells rang in my head as if I was about to enter a hitherto unexplored and possibly dangerous path. I assured her that iced water would be excellent and we sat for what was a good meal.

The conversation was progressing through the usual range of topics when I became suspicious that my host was surreptitiously directing us towards religious matters: having done it myself on occasions I recognized what was happening. Intrigued by this development I allowed the conversational drift to continue until I asked,

'Well, what is your religious conviction?'

'We're Mormons,' they responded enthusiastically. At that I clearly asked the right question when I enquired what they stood for and a lengthy explanation was given, supported by a number of scriptural references. As they continued, I realized that many of the scriptures were incorrectly quoted and much that was said was simply unbiblical. Increasingly I corrected my host's commentary until it occurred to him that I too had read the Bible.

'Hey,' he said, 'you know more than you're telling me. What's your story?'

At that I replied, 'Well I'll declare my hand by telling you of an experience I've had.' I told him how I had seen my wife come to the Lord, how I had met Jesus and how the orientation of my life had been changed. They drank in every word and as I finished Gerry immediately asked,

'What are you doing tomorrow evening?'

'I don't know,' I replied. 'You are the host and set out my diary.'

'Right,' the authoritative air-force officer was now taking command. 'You will have dinner with us and then speak to our church telling about your experience with God.' At that he went to the telephone in the next room to call his bishop and make the arrangements.

Gerry's house was of a typical American open-plan design, rooms being separated by arches but with no doors. I therefore couldn't help but hear Gerry's part of the telephone call.

'George,' he said. 'I want to tell you something exciting. I've got a man at my house having dinner with me and, George, this man has had an experience with God. He's got an incredible story to tell. We've got to get him to church to tell all our people. This is most important.' There was a long pause as George was evidently responding.

'But George . . .' Gerry sounded appealing. 'But George . . . you mean you won't . . . .?' Now his voice was rising in anger as he kept interrupting George's part of the conversation, fortunately hidden for all time from my ears.

'You what . . . you what . . . you *what*?' By now Gerry was shouting. 'Then I'll do it myself!' and with that I heard the telephone slammed down.

Gerry returned and was clearly on the boil. He snapped at his wife.

'George won't arrange a meeting because the whole church is going ten-pin bowling. Ten-pin bowling . . .' he added in despair, but his voice tailed off as half-formed ideas took shape.

'No they aren't. I'm going down to that bowling alley tomorrow evening and I'm getting every one of them out of there and I'm bringing them to a meeting!' And this he did.

There was one complication, however. The next morning I was being escorted between scientific meetings on the huge airbase and research complex when I met one of several expatriate Britons who were working there and whom I had encountered during the visit.

'Roy,' said my friend. 'All the Brits have decided to have a party in your honour since you're here and it's been arranged for tonight. We'll pick you up from your hotel at about 8.00 p.m.'

I thanked him for the thought, but then asked anxiously, 'Have you cleared this with Gerry? He's looking after my diary and I've an idea he's arranged something for the evening.'

As my friend went to look for Gerry I mused upon what I would do if the choice were put to me. The thought of a party in my honour was much more appealing to my senses than talking about Jesus to a church full of hard-nosed Mormons, but I knew if the choice was mine I would have to decide to go to the Mormon church.

In due course the party organizer returned to say that Gerry had indeed made an arrangement which he was not prepared to cancel but that a compromise had been worked out: Gerry would have me until 8.00 p.m. and the party would claim me from 8.00 p.m. onwards.

At the family dinner that evening I drank my iced water wondering what would happen. Gerry left the table to drive down to the bowling alley to collect the faithful and just before 7.00 p.m. we assembled. On the hour and following a brief introduction I was invited to speak on my experience of meeting with God. For an hour I shared with a most attentive audience, hanging on to every word as they learned that a real Jesus was able to communicate, challenging and changing lives, giving hope for the future. There came a point when I felt from within that the moment had come to stop. I did so, asking people to bow their heads in prayer and, as we knew the presence of the Lord in the silence that followed, invited him to touch and change every heart open to him.

As I said 'Amen' terminating the prayer, the front-door bell rang and glancing at my watch, I saw that it was precisely 8.00 p.m.

My hosts for the latter part of the evening whisked me away from this wide-eyed audience and in minutes I was sat in the very worldly surroundings of a party. The jovial level of the conversation was now entirely different, but soon friendships were being established and I was discovering a taste for smoked oysters, caviar and other delicacies.

However, I was very tired, so I wasn't sorry to see the

party begin to break up at about midnight. Soon I was
filing my way past our hosts, shaking hands with them
and thanking them for the delightful time. I had said
my thanks when my hosts, who I'd never met before,
commented, 'You know, we've noticed this evening that
there is something about you that is different. What is
it?'

The general hubbub of the disintegrating party,
friends bidding their good-nights to one another, suddenly became a pregnant silence as I replied,

'Well, I've met Jesus.'

All eyes were turned on me.

'Do tell us about it.' In an instant the trivial pursuits of
the evening were brushed aside as everybody filed back
into the room, sat down and all eyes were again filled
with enquiry and interest.

For the second time that evening, I related the reality
I had found in Jesus and how he had intervened in my
life. My audience, scientists and their wives, listened intently and a little after 2.00 a.m. a thoughtful group of
people left to go home.

I was driven back to my hotel by a man who continued
to ask questions, and as we stopped in the hotel car park
he turned to me, blurting out the story of his broken
life, hitherto known to no one. So it was that at 3.00 a.m. I
finished the Ohio leg of my itinerary with the US
government, praying in the car park with one of its scientists that the Lord Jesus, who had transformed my life,
would also transform his.

On my return home from this first American trip, the
aircraft was approaching Heathrow Airport when I felt
the Lord telling me I would return twice a year. This is
what happened for several years after that, as research
commitments drew me back to the USA and Canada.

Eventually the conviction grew within me that, instead
of crowding my time abroad with both business and spiritual commitments, it was the right thing to commit myself
to some itineraries that were entirely for Christian work.

With a response to this challenge there was once more
a fear of a new unknown and on my next journey, flying

to Montreal and then on to Ottawa, I realized that things were different. Hitherto my briefcase had always contained my Bible in one compartment with engineering papers in another and, subconsciously, this had been a sort of safety net. If I was to make a mess of a Christian meeting I knew that I could explain that I was really a scientist offering myself for the odd bit of Christian work, and I could then retire to the haven of my engineering. This time, there was no fall-back position: if the first meeting in Ottawa was a failure there were three to four weeks of similar meetings ahead.

A voice inside seemed to be taunting me as the aircraft cruised at 39,000 feet over the Atlantic Ocean: 'Who do you think you are; Great Britain's answer to Billy Graham? What makes you think you can pretend to be a man of God?'

If I could have opened the door of the aircraft and walked home I would have done.

In Ottawa, I was taken to a hotel for the night. My room was so splendid that I thought perhaps I ought not to sleep: it would be a waste of money not to be looking at such opulent surroundings.

In a very few hours I was collected to go to the early-morning prayer meeting, passing hundreds of people arriving for the main meeting. I was terrified. Then the time came to speak and, after sharing for a while, to give a challenge. In surprise I saw people beginning to come forward for counselling, the counselling rooms filling up, all the literature for counsellors used up, counsellors with queues of people around them and prayer continuing until 2.00 p.m. in a meeting that began at 7.00 a.m. It was my realization that a small step of faith in undertaking this itinerary had already resulted in a substantial blessing. In due course, this led to regular international trips whose sole objective was Christian work. Meanwhile my research was developing and so were consultancy contacts around the world. Papers were being presented at scientific conferences and, apart from the fact that the day did not seem long enough, everything seemed well set for the future. I had become highly

mobile both in my scientific and Christian work and the
word shared by that pastor a few years before had certainly come to pass.

The mobility, as it increased with time, brought increasing problems of separation from the family and the
Lord chose a trip to Canada to speak to me in this.

I had landed in Toronto, rather expecting a full itinerary to be waiting. Instead, my host pointed me to a car
telling me that I was to drive to a cabin on the shore of
Lake Huron, a couple of hundred miles north and there
I was to have a free weekend.

'But what about meetings: is nothing arranged?' I
asked.

'It's Queen Victoria's birthday,' he replied flatly. I
wasn't sure if he was talking to me in a mysterious code
or just joking, but what Queen Victoria had to do with
my itinerary I just couldn't work out. I then learned that
Canada still remembered the great Queen and had an
official holiday to honour her — and this was it.

I set off to Penatangsheen where I found the cabin
with my cheerful hosts. Fred insisted that we go fishing,
something that had always seemed to me to be remarkably dull. Even the fact that I had no equipment did not
deter him, boots, rods and all the gear appearing from
nowhere. We got into a small boat, and were propelled
by an outboard motor about a hundred yards off-shore.
Fred switched off the motor, tossed out his line, put his
feet on the gunwhales of the boat, leant back, slipped his
hat down over his eyes and, apparently, promptly went
to sleep. Agitated, I threw in my line and pulled it out
again. The worm was still there, unaccompanied by a fish.

Ten minutes of casting and reeling in and I'd had
enough fishing for a lifetime. Longingly, I looked from
the cockleshell on which I was perched, in which there
wasn't even room to pace up and down, towards the
shore. A hundred yards of water separated me from all
the things I wanted to do and with envy I thought of
those in the Bible to whom that was no barrier at all:
they would have just walked across. My musings were
broken by Fred's voice and then he began to minister

to me. I saw that the frenetic activity of my life, fulfilling as it was in itself, was denying me my main ministry — and that was to my family. From that time I took a different view of that responsibility.

★ ★ ★

The work had continued to increase though, and the pattern of events was highly satisfying. I was containing my Christian work in such a way that I could define my objectives and know where I was going, but this well-ordered layout was to be disturbed by a further pebble in the pond: an invitation to become associated with a post-graduate university in the USA by taking a professorial chair there. Of course, this is a career objective for people in academia, and for me was made particularly enriching because my whole time was to be spent on pursuing research topics. This made it possible to maintain my faculty position in the British academic institute with which I'd been for some years and in which I'd built my own research laboratory. There were now consultancies with several major corporations and I was invited to act as an adviser to government departments of several countries. In the USA I was now a federal government employee, paid for by the navy and working, in the main, with the air force and the army. Much travelling was involved and every few weeks time would be spent in the United Kingdom with my team of physicists, engineers and mathematicians who comprised the workers in my UK research programmes.

Just as all the opportunities to consolidate the career that had thus formed were before me, a series of circumstances arose that were outside my predictions for the future. Elizabeth and I prayed much about this. The more we looked into the future, the more uncertain it was and the less we realized we knew. We knew so little that, to make plans was ludicrous and we could only turn for instruction to the One who already knew what the future contained.

When it came, we couldn't believe it. 'Resign,' said the

Lord. I fought the prospect, asking and asking again, while doing all I could to change the circumstances that brought the question. The only answer we ever got was 'Resign' so, after six months of agonizing before the Lord, with a heavy heart, I resigned.

There was a three-month waiting period before the resignation became effective: hardly time to wind up affairs as I wanted to, and then came the first day free of the scientific life that had enthralled me, fulfilled me and taken every moment that I would give it. Elizabeth and I caught an aeroplane from California to Ontario, Canada, to lead a mission and after landing in Toronto, we drove to Kingston, Ontario.

It was autumn, the fall, a time of excitement and change and fallen leaves underfoot. That was when every new venture had begun in my life and now, the familiar, disturbing feeling inside of a quest to a new unknown, was there again. This was not a path to be trodden in my wisdom, for my wisdom had been shown to be foolishness to God. This would have to be a walk of faith, foolishness in the eyes of the world, but the only way to know the wisdom of God. It would be an even more tenuous trail than any I had previously trodden, but this time I knew that there was One who had gone ahead.

.

'Let no man deceive himself. If any man among you seemeth to be wise in this world, let him become a fool, that he may be wise. For the wisdom of this world is foolishness with God'

1 Corinthians 3:18-19